10r

THESE REMAIN
A Personal Anthology

THESE REMAIN

A Personal Anthology

Sir John Slessor

Memories of Flying,
Fighting and Field Sports

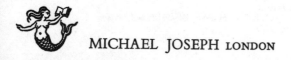
MICHAEL JOSEPH LONDON

First published in Great Britain by
MICHAEL JOSEPH LTD.
26 Bloomsbury Street
London, W.C.1
1969

© *1969 by Sir John Slessor*

Set and printed in Great Britain by
Ebenezer Baylis & Son Ltd., The Trinity Press, Worcester, and London
and bound by James Burn, Esher

7181 0656 3

To my grandchildren
ROBIN, JAMES, DAVID, ANTHONY *and* CATHERINE,
*on whom and on whose generation I am sure we can
rely for the future greatness of this country*

ACKNOWLEDGEMENTS

Thanks are due to the following for permission to reproduce material in which they hold the copyright: Cassell & Co. Ltd., London WC1, for permission to use *Prelude to Dunkirk 1940* and *The Tragedy of Warsaw* from THE CENTRAL BLUE by Sir John Slessor; Edward Arnold (Publishers) Ltd., London W1, for permission to use an extract from AVIATION IN PEACE AND WAR by Sir Frederick Sykes; The Executors of the Estate of the late Vita Sackville-West for permission to use an extract from her book THE LAND; Oxford University Press, London W1, for permission to use an extract from AIR POWER AND ARMIES by Sir John Slessor; Hamish Hamilton Ltd., London WC1, for permission to use an extract from THE DIPLOMACY OF GREAT POWERS by Sir William Hayter.

The following chapters were originally published as listed:

Trenchard and the birth of the RAF in the *Royal United Service Institution Journal*, August 1942

Porter: Artois, 1917 in the *RAF Quarterly*

Conky: India, 1922 in *Country Life*, 13th November 1958.

Pin: Rod, Saddle and Gun, 1923–1953 in *Country Life*, 27th August 1953.

When Soldiering Was Really Soldiering: Aldershot, 1925–1928 in *Time and Tide*.

Wilfrid Freeman and the Tools of Victory, 1940 in *The Listener*.

CONTENTS

1*

Introduction

The year 1968 saw the fiftieth anniversary of the Royal Air Force—of the date when the old Royal Flying Corps and Royal Naval Air Service were merged, not without some confusion and controversy, into one autonomous Air Service, the first in the world.

In connection with that occasion, I felt, as one who has had the good fortune to be among that now diminishing band who was a Serving Officer on 1 April 1918, and for some three years before that in the old R.F.C., that it might be worth putting together a miscellany of memories—some of which had already been published in other books and in various journals—to illustrate the kind of life led, and adventures enjoyed (though in some cases that is hardly the right word), by many of us old boys who lived through that period. I thought it might bring back to them some nostalgic memories; and hoped it might also interest and amuse some among younger generations, officers still serving, cadets and even younger men and boys in universities and schools—might even help to convince some of them that a career in the R.A.F. has still much to be said for it.

Of course, life in the Services has undergone immense changes since the days between the wars, and will change still more if or when the unhappy day comes when we shall have pulled out our garrisons from East of Suez. But life in the R.A.F. especially will still hold out great attractions and opportunities for seeing the world, and for adventure—including of course the great adventure of Service flying. It will by no means be confined to garrison duties in England.

As will be seen, many of my happiest memories are of field sports, particularly fly-fishing and fox-hunting. I was lucky enough to be young when this sort of thing was within the range of officers with limited means—and kind friends. It would be absurd to pretend that they are not far less so today. But other things are available to take their place, such as sailing, gliding, private flying, golf, tennis, cricket and rugger, for those who are prepared (as some of us were) to deny themselves other luxuries. Perhaps among the latter I should include the luxury of a far too early marriage; there is something in the old saying "Don't get married till you are in a position to support a wife, unless you are lucky enough to find a wife who is in a position to support you"—not so easy in these days of penal taxation. And it cannot be claimed that the present much higher pay, allowances, pensions, terminal grants and so-on, have compensated fully for the far higher cost of living than in the 'twenties and 'thirties. Nevertheless, the officer who is determined to enjoy life outside the bounds of duty can still do so, and many do—and the Service helps him to do so.

The chapter on "Trenchard and the Birth of the Royal Air Force" is in a rather different category from the rest, having been written for the R.U.S.I. Journal as a review of Mr. Boyle's excellent book on Trenchard. I include it as giving some picture of that great man whom I knew so well, and in particular of his attitude towards the creation of the R.A.F., which is often misunderstood—and, indeed, sometimes maliciously misrepresented.

No book of memories like this would be complete without something about Hitler's war—though that was a period that perhaps most of us would prefer to forget. I included the chapter on Wilfrid Freeman, not only because it reminds us of something that should not be forgotten, but also because Wilfrid, who was among my most intimate friends, was also I think one of the greatest of Air Force officers, whose name and immense achievements are far too little known. I have selected from my book *The Central Blue* two extracts—"Prelude to Dunkirk" and "The Tragedy of Warsaw"—as being, I think, especially dramatic episodes with which I was intimately connected, and of which again the details are not very well known to any but students of military history.

Apart from some passing references in the Epilogue, I have not included anything about my life since World War II, mainly because I did not feel that my experiences since then really lend themselves to a book of this sort. But (on instructions from my publisher) I append the following short summary.

When my friend and fellow Old-Haileyburian, Sir Trafford Leigh-Mallory, was killed early in 1945 in a crash on his way to assume the Air Command in South-East Asia, I was given the choice of taking his place or coming home from Italy to take up the job of Air Member for Personnel, which I knew the C.A.S. had wished me to do. I know I should have enjoyed the Far East Command but I had already had two good Commands-in-Chief, Coastal and Mediterranean/Middle East; I knew the war could not go on much longer and I felt I could serve the R.A.F. better by becoming A.M.P. I cannot say I looked forward to it with much pleasurable anticipation—but it was a challenge. It would involve a leading part in the unhappy task of breaking down the great war-time Air Force and the more congenial one of building up a peace-time Force in its place. Above all, it would include the job of demobilization—and I was old enough to remember the difficulties in that connection twenty-six years earlier. We had our difficulties all right, due in no small degree to the inevitable sensation-mongering in certain sections of the popular Press; but on the whole it went relatively smoothly. I had not reckoned with the very efficient demobilization scheme drawn up under the supervision of Mr. Ernest Bevin who told me himself how much he owed to the unique experience in Personnel matters of Air Vice-Marshal Sir John Cordingley, the Director-General of Manning at the Air Ministry. John held my hand in Kingsway, and I'm sure prevented me from doing too many silly things as A.M.P.

There followed in 1948 and 1949 the job of Commandant of

the Imperial Defence College. That was very interesting and relatively easy, being free from any real burden of responsibility; "a faulty strategic decision in an exercise at the I.D.C. involves no unnecessary widows," as my predecessor, Bill Slim, used to say. At the same time one kept in the closest touch with developments in Defence policy. I still believe it to be an ideal prelude to becoming one of the Chiefs of Staff, and think it a pity that Slim and I are the only two who have enjoyed that advantage.

Then at the end of 1949 I was lucky enough (and this sort of thing always involves a large element of luck) to be selected for the post of Chief of the Air Staff by Mr. Attlee. Probably few people realize how very much the appointment of Chiefs of Staff depends on the decision of the Prime Minister; and I am sure Attlee's decision was in no way influenced by the fact that he too was a devoted Old Haileyburian! I suppose every Chief of Staff likes to feel that his period of office was particularly exacting. It would be silly to pretend that mine was a soft job, but I think some of my successors have had—and are having— a more arduous and difficult time than I had. Features of my period were the early build-up of NATO, the Korean war and the consequent enormous expansion scheme for the R.A.F.— including the decision on the nuclear V-Bombers—and a massive study of Future Allied Strategy for the Cabinet, which I was sent to discuss and agree with the American Chiefs of Staff. There was no Chief of the Defence Staff in those days. In the interest of continuity we agreed that one should represent the three of us at the numerous NATO meetings, in Washington and other capitals, and as a rule that job fell to me for some two years. It was, of course, all intensely interesting but I was not altogether sorry to see the end of it. Mr. Churchill, on his return to power in October 1951 was not the easiest of men to work under and he did not particularly care for me. So it was with some relief that at the end of 1952 I handed over my chair to another old friend and rather younger contemporary at Haileybury, Dickie Dickson, and left Whitehall for what I fondly, and quite erroneously, imagined would be a quiet and leisurely life in Somerset.

As a matter of fact I do not think I was at that age the sort of chap who could be content with leading a quiet and lazy life in the country, and my anticipation has in no way been fulfilled. There is an arrangement—which actually is not altogether just an amiable fiction—that Marshals of the R.A.F. and their equivalents in the other Services never retire but remain serving officers for the rest of their lives (unfortunately the idea in some quarters that they also draw full pay for the rest of their lives is a myth!); so I have been able to keep in fairly close touch with the Service and, I hope, occasionally to be of some little use. I have written a number of books and innumerable articles on War and Defence policy generally, and have lectured on these subjects in many Defence Colleges, Universities and to private audiences at home and abroad, on both sides of the Atlantic. Apart from that my principal activities have been in connection with the Commonwealth and the development of the Atlantic Community.

But all that is largely over now; a time comes when one is too old and out of touch with current affairs to go on airing one's opinion, except to a very limited extent; and increasing lameness makes it difficult for me to lead as active a life as I used to. For the future I must, in the main, content myself with making myself as useful as may be and keeping out of mischief by taking as active a part as I can in local County affairs, and looking back with thankfulness upon a long and, on the whole, happy life in the wider field.

J.C.S.

1   The Spring Begins, 1907–1917

A discussion of Siegfried Sassoon's works heard recently on the wireless sent me back to his *Memoirs of a Fox-Hunting Man* which, with other old favourites, lives on my bedside table. He always wrote beautifully, whether in prose or poetry, and of his War he wrote with knowledge, strength and compassion. But there are others I think as good on that subject—Edmund Blunden for instance, and Mottram's *Spanish Farm* trilogy which, more than anything I know, brings back to me with luminous clarity the sights and sounds and smells—the very climate and atmosphere—of the vast, grim siege that was the Western Front in Flanders fifty years ago.

But I have always loved the *Fox-Hunting Man*, not only for its style and content[1] but also because it brings to life for me buried memories of that serene, secure world that I too am old enough to remember—the world that passed when the lights went out in 1914. Sassoon's simple, modest story of fox-hunting and point-to-point racing in the "Ringwell" country has, too, a special appeal to me because I also loved fox-hunting and moreover, used to hunt in that same country in which I sometimes spent short leaves staying with an old 21st Lancer cousin in a rather ugly Victorian mansion, where from the billiard-room windows one could see "Basset Wood". That was after Denis Milden's day as Master. But when I first read the *Fox-Hunting Man* in its first edition I was able to identify, with Charles's help, the real names, not only of villages and coverts, but of Sassoon's people still going strong—old Colonel Hesmon, Farmer Pacey and his good bob-tailed cob, Arthur

---

[1] He once showed me the original manuscript of the *Fox-Hunting Man* (his first book) in his neat handwriting with hardly a deletion or amendment— So different from my own effort, which often runs through several drafts.

Brandwick, and Bob Millet in his stained hunting cap and with a pipe always between his teeth, even out hunting. The book still recalls to me how heavy the Weald could ride in wet winters, and how lovely it looked from above on a clear day when hounds met up on the Downs and we would start by drawing one of those gorse coverts that so often held a fox.

★   ★   ★

One way in which I have something in common with Sassoon —though I was never nearly as good a horseman as he was—is that my greatest joy in fox-hunting was galloping over fences. As I grew older and more experienced, I was able to appreciate good hound work and enjoy watching a wise huntsman quietly handling his pack—casting them when necessary but patiently letting them work out their own line, refusing to pick them up and hustle them to any holloa there might be or any lifted hat on the sky-line. More than once I have wondered at the ability of a huntsman to recognize those lifted hats at a distance, "oh no, that's old so-and-so, he wouldn't know a hunted fox if he saw one". And, now I come to think of it, how phonetically inexact the word "Holloa" is; nothing could be less descriptive of that shrill, eldritch scream (which, incidentally, I could never manage) that so often speeded my pulse as a whipper-in from a vantage point beyond the covert viewed a fox away.

But hound-work in itself without jumping fences was never enough for me; which is why, I am not ashamed to say, I always loved a Drag. The Swallowfield line, the "Arm of the Sea",[2] and the line that ended over that huge *nullah* in Easthampstead Park; the line between the Wargrave road and Hawthorn Hill where one could have the clean, black fences as

---

[2] A Drag-line so called to commemorate an incident when the airmen from Andover and the sailors from Greenwich, at Camberley for a Combined Operations exercise, were having a ride on borrowed horses. A kindly soldier sang out, "Put on a bit of steam at this one—there's a bit of a brook on the far side"; and a sailor as he landed safely, "Bit of a brook by God! I call it a bloody Arm of the Sea."

they came without worrying about marking flags, and the big timber somewhere between Ascot and Bracknell, of which a rather intimidating footnote on the Drag notice-board read "only officers with good horses should ride this line". How one does forget those names which were so much the spice of life at Camberley half a life-time ago. We got so much care-free amusement out of the Drag. One day in particular sticks in my memory. There was a freezing fog, and some had their doubts about throwing off; but it was the last day of a Staff College year, and said the Master, Major Barry de Fonblanque, R.A. "it's the last line the old Senior Division chaps will have—we'd better have a go". So we had a go, galloping blind to the cry of invisible hounds throwing their tongues a field or two ahead, not seeing the fences till we were within a few yards of them. At the check someone admiringly chaffed the Master for jumping a five-bar gate, at which he confessed that the fog had frozen on his spectacles and he'd thought it was an ordinary post and rails; fortunately he was riding that great old horse War Baby, on which he had show-jumped for England some years before. And down in a corner of the field, hidden in the fog, hounds were baying a Scots Captain (later a commander of the Highland Division) who had been running with the "smell", and had taken refuge up a pollarded willow-tree.

What fun it all was! Not but that a good day at the real thing was still more thrilling—a quick burst with hounds streaming away on a breast-high scent, the gay high-pitched laughter of the horn that quickens the blood, and the absorbing pleasure of cutting out one's own line on a good horse over big country. And if you were lucky enough to be up with them at the end of a long hunt, what was there to equal the feeling of proud satisfaction as you threw a leg over his withers and slid from the saddle to smack a steaming neck and tell yourself how clever you had been? And then the warm content of hacking home unbuttoned in the gathering dusk, chewing the cud of memory. All that comes back to me from the pages of Sassoon's book, as when an old dance tune heard on the wireless recalls the happy nights of youth—pink coats and programme cards, and bones and beer at four in the morning.

I was never up to pig-sticking, which I can well believe was *the* incomparable horseman's game; having two gammy legs (the result of polio as a child) and so no grip, I could not spare a hand for a spear. For the same reason I was never any good at polo; I used to play in India and loved it; but some strokes—a near-side back-hander in particular—were impossible for me; the quick snatch at a sort of suit-case handle sewn to the saddle-bow, which kept me firmly in the plate over fences, was no substitute for the grip with knees and thighs that enables a man to lean far enough out to one side or the other for a difficult shot. But I was able to enjoy my hunting to the full—and incidentally got a lot of fun out of hunter trials in the Staff College team with three horse-gunners who were kind enough to ask me to join them, I am sure only because I was lucky enough to have a couple of very good horses who were onward bound and enjoyed jumping fences as much as I did. The one thing one can not do without grip is cram a horse at a fence if he does not want to have it; I remember shooting like a cork out of a bottle clean over one obstacle in a Garth point-to-point when a little horse of mine, who had never before been known to turn his head, for some unaccountable reason decided at the last moment that he was not for it.

*   *   *

How one does drool on when once started about fox-hunting! The real reason I originally put pen to this paper is that, on re-reading the *Fox-Hunting Man*, I found this time that what made a special appeal to me was the author's affection for the friends of his youth; because—curiously enough—as I grow older my feeling about my own greatest boyhood friend, also killed in the Great War, instead of waning seems to grow stronger.

"Someone informed me that Sergeant Dixon had died of pneumonia"—just that, stark and without comment, about his old groom who had taught him to ride and love hunting, and was serving as a Transport Sergeant in another Division; somehow that strikes me as almost the most poignant line in the book. But of course it was the deaths of Stephen Colwood and Dick Tiltwood that hit Sassoon hardest; Stephen, the boyhood friend of blissful hunting seasons in Sussex before the war; and Dick of whom I feel, from the author's account of that visit to C Company's dug-out in the Line, that he must have had the premonition of death that I have known come to some in war with absolute, unquestioned certainty.[3] In spite of—or perhaps, because of—his admirable economy of words, Sassoon's love for those two shines like a lamp from his pages. And I have known something very similar, though I don't think I ever had his warmly sensitive depth of feeling—and certainly not his ability to express it so well, without false sentiment or vain repining.

Looking back on a long and crowded life in which I have been blessed with wonderful friends, of whom all too many have died in two World Wars (of the forty-six boys in my House at Haileybury in 1913, twenty were dead within five years, and many of my friends in the Services were killed) I often think it strange that the one above all to whose loss I have never been able to reconcile myself is the boy who was my boon companion in the years before the Kaiser's war. I still have only to close my eyes to see him and hear his voice as clearly as if he was in the room with me, though he has been gone these fifty years, killed as a gunner subaltern in the Ypres Salient. He was Revere Osler, so christened after his direct ancestor Paul Revere of the American War of Independence, but for some unknown reason always called Tom, or Tommy —I suspect because he felt that Revere was a bit too much of a good thing.

★   ★   ★

One hesitates to use the word "beautiful" about a young man, but I really think it is the only word to describe his appearance

---

[3] Sassoon, shortly before he died, told me he thought this was so. See Chapter 10.

—and his manners and whole bearing, for that matter; he was in fact anything but effeminate and I'm sure would have resorted to physical violence if I had ever used it of him in his hearing. But I remember my feeling, as a tough, rather insensitive little boy, of almost awestruck admiration of his good looks—and he was one of those rare beautiful people who are just as nice as they look. He was tall, fair hair springing rather far back on his forehead, very clear grey eyes and a skin of that healthy pallor that never seems to take a tan. And his hands were like those of a great sculptor or pianist—the only hands I have ever known in a man to compare with his are those of General Omar Bradley of the U.S. Army who, dear old boy, was certainly no Adonis in other ways.

Tommy was an astonishingly clean boy; he was ready to participate in any schoolboy rag but was unobtrusively fastidious, and one never saw him grubby or with stockings round his ankles as I so often was; he contrived somehow always to smell of good soap and Harris tweed. I think it speaks volumes for him that my affection was undimmed by my admiration and my awareness that he was always able to do things better than I could, and with more unselfconscious ease. I'm sure that subconsciously I was always trying to live up to his standard, but he was such an essentially nice boy that it never made me feel jealous or resentful—and I suppose I was not much of a one for inferiority complexes.

His voice was very slightly hoarse, with a trace of accent derived from his Canadian father, the famous physician, and his stately American mother both of whom I adored. They must surely have got pretty sick of me—I was always in and out of their house—but they never showed it and were the soul of kindness (by the way, how unfortunate are modern boys in getting tipped only in bank-notes on their birthdays; a bit of crumpled paper can never engender quite the same thrill as those little gold coins of bygone days). I have never felt as sad for anyone as I did for those two when their only child was killed. With him their light went out and actually neither of them survived him very long. Lady Osler left me in her will a massive oak chest alleged to have belonged to her famous great-grandfather. She was a darling and I think understood me, and I her, even better than my own mother. A big, handsome woman with immense natural dignity—a vintage *grande-dame*—but with a vivid sense of humour she treated her husband, who was one of the great wits of his day, with a sort of rather scandalized amusement at the outrageous things he was sometimes wont to say. One summer (was it 1911?) a protégé of Sir William's, a rising young doctor named Harvey Cushing, was married from their house in Norham Gardens and the young couple left that evening in (I think) the *Mauretania* for New York.[4] Next day, as so often, I was lunching with the Oslers (I remember we had grapefruit to start with, a great novelty in England in those days) when a servant came in with a telegram for her. "Oh my my," she said, "the bride (I forget her name) has left all her nighties behind here." Sir William, with a perfectly solemn face, "What does she want with nighties on her honeymoon?" And she, twinkling, "*William!* Not in front of the boys." I don't suppose I then had any idea of what he meant, but the episode has stuck in my mind as so characteristic of that beloved couple.

Theirs was, I think, the happiest household I ever knew in those days before the Madness. The big house in Oxford (where, of course, Sir William was Regius Professor of Medicine) with its wide high rooms, old furniture and polished oak floors, seemed always to be full of sunshine from the garden at the back, and forms the background of what are still among the most delightful memories of my life.

*   *   *

The Oxford of my early youth seems in retrospect almost unbelievably remote from the place where to-day there is

---

[4] One of their daughters, Betsey, is the wife of Jock Whitney. When he was Ambassador in London she introduced me to her grandchildren, who were staying with them in that vast Residence in Regent's Park. Having been at her parents' wedding, that made me feel rather old.

sometimes a solid jam of cars and 'buses and lorries from Magdalen Bridge to Carfax. Horse trams still clanked down the High and hansom cabs waited for fares in St. Aldates—their horses wore straw hats in high summer and tossed their nose-bags, scattering grain on the cobbles of the cab-stand to the delight of the Oxford sparrows. The Italian organ grinder, with his little monkey in red coat and pill-box cap, played "All the Little Pansy Faces" and "Daisy, Daisy" in the Bardwell road, to the distraction of us struggling with Long Division or Caesar's conquest of Gaul in what was not yet called the Dragon School. The muffin man rang his bell on grey winter afternoons. And a Mr. Morris[5] kept a little bicycle shop some-where near Magdalen.

Winter was fun. There was skating on the flooded meadows downstream of the Barges; Ronnie Poulton—a famous Old Dragon and one of the finest three-quarters that ever played for England—scoring tries for the Varsity on the Iffley road ground; sometimes even a visitation from Olympian heroes like the All Blacks; members of the Bullingdon in mud-splashed pink coats cracking hunting whips in Tom Quad to the disgust of Mr. Sidney Owen;[6] and everywhere young men in shorts and sweaters with great scarfs round their necks walked or bicycled between their colleges and the innumerable playing fields. Phil Wroughton (killed at first Gaza) or Kerr Fraser-Tytler coming to tea on wet Sunday evenings—crum-pets and a little spirit lamp under the silver tea kettle in the drawing room; the cheerful din and bustle of St. Giles's Fair, the lights of Elliston's windows gleaming on rain-splashed pavements in the Cornmarket, the delicious smell of roasting coffee as one passed the Cadena, and a useful but unglamorous household utensil crowning the Martyrs' Memorial—perhaps it is all much the same to-day, but somehow I doubt it.

But it was in the summer holidays that Oxford was at its best. The garden of our house on the Iffley road ran down to the

[5] The late Lord Nuffield.
[6] A famous Classical Don of the House.

Christ Church cricket ground, and we looked out on to an expanse of smooth turf and beyond to the trees of Christ Church Meadows—hardly another building in sight. We could watch cricket from the lawn, and one unforgettable year the Australians played some English side on the House ground— my parents gave a garden party for the occasion, the ladies with tight waists in long sweeping dresses and floppy picture hats and the men in flannels with straw boaters or Panamas. I wonder why the summer weather of one's youth always seems in retrospect to have been so much better than it usually is now. It was while watching cricket with Tommy from that lawn in 1912 that I heard a curious humming sound and saw my first aeroplane sailing sedately against a background of great white clouds beyond the trees to southward.

*   *   *

I don't know—perhaps people of my generation tend to be unduly sentimental about the friends of our distant youth, those golden young men who died in their thousands in the holocausts of 3rd Ypres and the Somme, and whose like their surviving contemporaries swear we shall never see again. I don't think I over-sentimentalize about Tom. I too was in France when he was killed but far away from him, down on the Arras front while he was up in the Salient. It did not have the impact on me that I would have expected; perhaps my sensitivity was blunted at the time by familiarity with death and the pressure of current experience which—while nothing to compare with what the poor devils in the trenches and battery positions had to put up with—was not conducive to the finer feelings. I loved him with an unselfish devotion of a kind I do not think I have known since for any man. But I did not weep for him, as I did for my youngest brother Tony, another keen fox-hunter who died with the 43rd Light Infantry in Burma between the Wars—and for my father, who survived Blackwater in West Africa and Yellow fever in Jamaica to die peacefully in my presence of some pneumonic infection in a London nursing home. Those were the only two occasions on which I have shed tears since, as a small boy, I often wept for more mundane reasons such as a whippy cane across that portion of my anatomy so admirably suited to the purpose—and once, I still recall with shame, bellowed from sheer funk when first introduced, at the age of about seven, to the big swimming bath under what is now called the Skipper Hall at the Dragon School.

★　★　★

Tommy and I were at that school together until he went on to Winchester and I to Haileybury, when we remained inseparable companions in the holidays. Looking back, I do not quite know why we were such close friends. We did not have all that many tastes in common—though the one above all that we did share amounted to a passion with both of us. With that notable exception he was not much interested in games or sport, though he seemed always to be busy and never short of something to do. We both liked drawing and I think had a real aptitude for it. Tommy's delicate pen and ink sketches of old houses—the Almshouses at Ewelme, for instance, where his father was Trustee—reflected his instinctive good taste. My own surviving efforts were not so demanding and, for the most part, depict less peaceful scenes; H.M.S. *Victory* under full sail with all guns blazing (or, to be more exact, smoking); very degenerate-looking Turkish soldiers in tarbushes fleeing from Italians in Bersagliere hats against a Libyan background of palm trees and minarets—strange to recall that there was battle in "The Desert" even in that day. Tom was a keen and good carpenter. And he amassed a fine collection of butterflies and moths—mainly rare moths, which he kept beautifully set in cork-lined boxes (how well I remember that camphor smell of the killing bottles). I could never work up much enthusiasm for that, but often lent a hand, doing my share of shinning up the lamp-posts of North Oxford to smear the glass with the sticky mixture of black treacle and molasses that trapped the night moths round the light—do small boys still do that? I wonder.

Tommy played the usual school games; he liked cricket and was a fair batsman—and he loved swimming and swam like a fish; but was always bored by football. I don't think he played golf—anyway I never played with him. That was a pity; it was a game I was very fond of. I was never any good—never took out a handicap, but certainly never got below about sixteen on my best day; still I played pretty regularly for many years and had a great deal of fun out of it. It occurs to me as I write that the first two occasions on which I fell in love were both on golf courses. The first was on the little windy links at Powfoot by the shore of the Solway Firth, when I was about 13; the second in the following year, with a beautiful, very blonde stranger (I now think probably old enough to be my mother—which, after all, was not very old) whom I encountered when setting out for a solitary game and who was kind enough to play several rounds with a rather callow schoolboy over that formidably good course at Sheringham; she was a very good golfer, I remember.

As far as I know Tom never threw a leg across a pony—I don't think horses came into his life at all, anyway until he became a gunner. And he did not care much for shooting; actually we were both too young to take it up seriously before the War overtook us, though I used to accompany my father to pheasant shoots at Bagley Wood and Waterperry, in charge of the cartridge bag and a portly liver-and-white spaniel named Taffy. I never shot game myself until 1915, when I bought a cheap 12-bore in Alexandria to shoot duck on Lake Mariut and guinea-fowl for the pot in the Sudan the following year. I doubt whether he would ever have gone in for it; he loved birds and the open country, and I think his was too gentle a nature to take kindly to shooting as a sport.

*   *   *

The one sport that Tommy really loved and was very good at —far better than I—was angling. I like that old-fashioned word with its Izaak Walton associations; and Sir Edward Grey[7] uses

---

[7] The late Lord Grey of Falloden, Foreign Secretary in 1914.

it in his delightful *Fly Fishing*, probably Tommy's favourite book of which his mother gave me his copy after his death. I have it by me now with, on the fly leaf in his neat and very mature handwriting, "E. R. Osler. January 19th 1910". He loved the sport itself but I think he also felt, as I do, that one of its greatest joys lies in the peaceful beauty of river scenery—the rushing rivers of Kashmir under the pines, brown lochs in the hills of Mull, the lazy quiet of Wiltshire chalk-streams waiting for the evening rise.

My most vivid memories of those pre-War days are nearly all of angling expeditions with Tommy. We fished with floats for perch and roach in Thames and Cherwell, but got bored with that when we had tasted higher things. We had a go at the renowned (but for me still mythical) Thames trout by the old Trout Inn at Godstow. We fished for chub in the side streams of the main river above Oxford—though the best place for that was where the stream ran out of the lake at Blenheim. Our main ploy there was spinning for pike in the lake in winter—a bitterly cold occupation, with ice forming in the rings of the rod. But there was a broad pool below the cascade, cleared of weed by the rush of water from the outflow drain, where on warm days one could see as many as a dozen big chub sunning themselves with their dorsal fins awash—very shy and hard to catch, being too far from the bank for me or any but a good fisherman to reach with a fly. But one hot afternoon in September 1912 I saw Tom drop a big black Palmer softly in the middle of them—a boil and a hurroosh and a 2½ pounder came to his net. That was the only time I remember seeing him use the dry fly; I was only introduced to that cream of the angler's sport six years later, on the Wiltshire Avon below the Central Flying School in the last summer of the War.

Our most memorable expeditions were both in the year of the Kaiser's War. That April we had a wonderful week in the Easter holidays on the Duff House beat of the Deveron, seven lovely pools whose names still thrill me—Bridge of Alvah, the

Duck pool, the Gullet, Coldwell, Blairie, Kirkside and the Tidal pool. The water was too low and clear to be any good for salmon (how often that seems to happen unless one lives by a salmon river), though they were showing themselves in a tantalizing fashion—probably mostly kelts. Tom had a 10-pounder from the Bridge pool and I in the top end of the Kirkside lost a smaller grilse, or perhaps a big sea-trout, actually at the net after playing him (no doubt too ham-handedly in my excitement) for about ten minutes; I was not far from tears that time. And in the Tidal pool one day when I was trying to get a long line out to a salmon moving under the far bank I caught a short-horn cow, behind me! I can still hear the scream of the reel as the affronted old girl gallumphed off across that big field in front of Duff House, tail erect and my nice new Silver Doctor embedded in some specially tender part of her anatomy, while Tommy stood and cried with helpless laughter.

But we caught in the week about 120 brown and sea-trout between us—Tommy, needless to say, more than I—and were blissful, fishing all day and returning to enormous dinners of good Scots cooking in our warm little pub on Low Street, Banff.

*   *   *

And then . . . our last expedition together, in the summer holidays; we hired a couple of Canadian canoes from Mr. Timms and, with a little tent and sleeping gear, set out to follow the "stripling Thames" to as near its source as we could get. That was a halcyon journey in the lovely cloudless weather of late July 1914—paddling slowly all day up that placid stream through the homely fields of Oxfordshire, cooking rather smoky meals of sausage and eggs and bacon over our wood fire beside the tent at night, and fishing in early mornings and late afternoons the little tributaries that feed the upper Thames. And we bathed—two or three times a day, unencumbered by clammy bathing dresses. We had both been introduced to that long before amid a squealing shoal of naked urchins in the Cherwell at the bottom of the Dragons' cricket field, under the watchful eye of old J.B. or the Tortoise.[8] Maybe for that reason I have always thought that—except perhaps for Caribbean lagoons or remote Mediterranean coves—a river, the right sort of river and especially the Cher at Oxford, is much the nicest place to swim in. Grass banks and the tangle of little coral-tinted roots beneath the surface by the fringe; cold, clear water and the green flash of weed swinging lazily far under one's feet; and Rupert Brooke's "thrilling-sweet and rotten unforgettable, unforgotten river-smell".

Then one morning in early August at a farm by the river somewhere up near Lechlade, where we had gone to buy milk and eggs, we were told that War had been declared—I suppose we must have seen something in the papers some weeks before about some unknown potentate who had been murdered at some place of which we had never heard; but the idea of war had never entered our heads. Anyway, that was the end of holidays for us—how much the end, we little knew. And we paddled hard downstream to a strange Oxford. The Schools being fitted out as a hospital; Reservists from the barracks at Cowley (wearing, as I remember, strange unblackened boots fresh from mobilization stores) marching down the High with heavy packs and slung rifles to entrain at the station; and, a portent, a couple of flying machines landing for no apparent reason on Port Meadow.

Our reactions to this thing that came upon us so unexpectedly were different. I was foolishly, though perhaps naturally, elated. Born with the Army in India of a family with a tradition of Military and Naval Service, educated at a school that had started as the nursery of the men who made British India, I had always taken it for granted—in an age when Kipling was writing *Recessional* and Elgar his *Land of Hope and Glory*—that wider still and wider would our bounds be set. As for war— well, that was something that did happen sometimes; was not my father away fighting a war on the North-West Frontier

[8] Mr. Martin and Mr. Haines, famous men at Mr. C. C. Lynam's Oxford Preparatory School in the early nineteen-hundreds.

when I was a baby? Tommy, on the other hand, hated the whole thing. It has occurred to me to wonder whether he too had one of those premonitions; but probably not. I think it was just that his whole family background and tradition were so different from mine; the world of international medicine and scholarship—that house in Norham Gardens was frequented by eminent doctors from far and wide; and the family's close association with America was unlikely to have engendered uncritical enthusiasm for Empire—though they were all three of them British subjects as loyal as they come. Tom was wholly ignorant of and uninterested in matters Military; and he so loved the happy life at Oxford, that he could not bear the thought of it all being horribly disrupted.

However, it was not long before he went off, first (his father's influence) as a medical orderly and later, thinking that employment inappropriate to a fit young man of his age, to a commission in the artillery. I—after a last term at Haileybury, some months of feverish lobbying of soldier relatives and friends of the family, and a few weeks trying (with little success) to remedy my total ignorance of the workings of a petrol engine in Mr. Morris's new garage in Longwall—squeezed in through the back door to the Royal Flying Corps (my application for a commission being marked in red ink by an indignant War Office Medical Board "permanently unfit for any form of Military Service").

*　　*　　*

Tommy and I never saw each other again.

I was in the Middle East for some time, and later our rare home leaves never coincided—I never saw him in uniform. We did not write often; we never had—did not need to, when we saw so much of each other. I don't think I even thought about him much; we were probably both too absorbed, in our different ways, with the strange new life of war in foreign lands to give much thought to old days when we had been so happy in each other's company. The next thing I knew, he was dead— mortally wounded with his battery in the Salient. And, by an extraordinary coincidence, the Medical Officer who tried vainly to save his life in that Dressing Station off the Menin road was the same man who had brought him into this world, in Canada twenty-one years before.

*   *   *

Well . . . there it is. I really set out to write about Tom, but seem to have written as much or more about myself. For that perhaps I may plead the excuse that the boy I was when he was alive, and the man I became as I grew up after he was killed, both owed something to his influence in our formative years. Some may feel that my picture of this quiet, gentle boy who was my friend makes him out too much of a paragon—a bit too good to be true. I don't know—how does one define a paragon? What I do know is that he was a very, *very* special sort of boy. And I would like younger generations of his family and mine, fifty years after his death, to know of him as something more than just another name on some Roll of Honour.

> ". . . time remembered is grief forgotten,
> And frosts are slain and flowers begotten,
> And in green underwood and cover
> Blossom by blossom the spring begins."
>   Swinburne

2 Let Us Now Praise Famous Men: Haileybury, 1911–1914

> . . . Ancients of the College
> For they taught us common sense—
> Tried to teach us common sense—
> Truth and God's Own Common Sense,
> Which is more than knowledge![1]

Schoolmasters are a remarkable breed of men—just how remarkable we seldom understand until we have left school and, looking back, realize belatedly how dedicated was their absorption in their job. There are, of course, some advantages in the career—perhaps particularly in that of a Master at a great Public School. Congenial companions with the same interests—on the whole probably a more congenial type of pupil than at other schools (though no doubt I shall be accused of being a snob for saying so); often noble buildings and beautiful surroundings in which to live and work; and good holidays at regular and predictable intervals—all this is true enough. But the material prospects for a young man taking up school-mastering after an expensive education are slender indeed, compared to those open to men of corresponding intelligence and capacity in other walks of life. Not for him the Peerages and knighthoods to which others may attain if they are really successful—and lucky. The financial rewards, though to-day better than they were of old, are still ludicrously small when set against those in most other professions. And for those of us who lack the vocation to teach (for vocation it is) it is difficult to comprehend how they can go on—term after term and year

[1] *A School Song* by Rudyard Kipling.

2

after year—coping with relays of often rather tiresome little boys, in the class-room, in the House and on the playing fields, throughout their waking hours—and still retain their sanity and sense of humour.

Nevertheless, I think they are to be envied. It is a constructive life—and a good life in which one is able to see for oneself, after not too long an interval of time, the fruits of one's labours. And who but schoolmasters can feel (though I doubt whether one in a hundred gives it a thought) that in, say fifty years' time, there will be scores of elderly gentlemen—Prime Ministers, Bishops and Judges, Ambassadors and Generals, Bankers and Captains of Industry—and just plain honest-to-God retired chaps living peaceably in their habitations, who will remember them with respect and often with affection?

> And their work continueth,
> Broad and deep continueth,
> Great beyond their knowing.

*   *   *

It is the fashion nowadays to abuse the Public Schools. There is in Parliament and Press a turgid outpouring of prejudiced nonsense, accusing them of being hot-beds of privilege and class distinction, exclusive preserves of the undeserving rich—and so-on and so-on. I do not think we need take all this too seriously, and from what I know of them the Public Schools do not,[2] though they are far more forward-looking and less complacent than most people give them credit for being. There are, after all, some things to be said for Democracy—and one of them is the freedom for people to talk drivel without others getting too worked up about it. But we who believe that the Public Schools have still an enormously valuable contribution

[2] Since this was written, the Public Schools have been shown to be fully justified in this attitude by the First Report of the Public Schools Commission (the Newsom Report) on which so much time and money has been squandered. It is a flop, if ever there was one. To me, of its two hundred and thirty-seven pages only six make any sense—those containing the note of dissent by three of its members and the note of reservation by a fourth.

to make to the progress and prosperity of our Country and its people should not allow this current clap-trap—born of jealousy out of ignorance—to go by default. We know what these great schools have done and are doing to turn out the type of man who in my young days governed, administered and defended the Empire (not so badly, after all), and who in these very different and more difficult times are as badly needed as ever—if not more so. We know above all that, in the words of Archbishop Lord Fisher of Lambeth, "their chief characteristic has been loyalty to some form of responsible service" and if there is anything more desperately needed in the Britain of to-day than that, I should like to know what it is.

This is not a treatise on the Public School system, but I must say two things about it. First, it is a fallacy to imagine (as many seem to do) that the Public Schools nourish class prejudice, and exercise what is called a "socially divisive influence". In fact they do no such thing. I must resist the temptation to enlarge unduly on this theme, but I wonder how many of this brand of critic knows that of the parents of boys now in the 160-odd Independent Schools in the Headmasters' Conference, only about a half were at any of those schools themselves. What is happening—and has been happening for generations—is that the son of a good "working-class" parent goes to a State School, gets a decent job when he leaves, works hard and makes some money and rises in the social scale—and then sends *his* son to a Public School. Thus, so far from having a socially divisive influence, these schools are having precisely the reverse effect—are making a really important contribution to what I believe is called Social Mobility; but they are doing it by gradual stages; and any attempt at an arbitrary short-cut to the same end would surely defeat its own object. One of the few Latin tags that remains with me since my days in the Lower Classical Sixth at Haileybury is "Si naturam expellas furca tamen usque recurret" —if you root out nature with a pitchfork, it will recoil on you. Nothing could be more surely calculated to have a socially disruptive effect than any move by a Government to legislate

against one of the fundamental freedoms of the British citizen—
the freedom, after paying his expensive share of the cost of
educating other people's children, to spend that diminishing
share of his own money left to him by the tax and rate collec-
tors on whatever he likes, including the form of education he
chooses for his own children.

Secondly, this form of criticism has its roots in the idea,
itself to a rapidly increasing extent a fallacy, that a Public
School education confers great material advantages in later life.
True, there are still a few vestigial advantages, which have very
little to do with "snob-value", in some professions; but they
are very few—and getting fewer. Anyway, I can never understand why this is anything of which we should be ashamed.
Why should the chap who runs a Jaguar on the never-never
system, spends his spare money in bars and betting shops and
leaves it to other people to pay for his children's education be
considered more socially admirable or of greater value to the
community than his neighbour, who is content with a second-
hand Mini and denies himself, not just luxuries but many of the
ordinary amenities, in order to give his son what he regards
as the best educational start in life? I find it hard to keep my
temper when I am told that the Public Schools are only for the
wealthy. Certainly there are a few schools to which only well-
to-do parents can afford to send their sons. But there are plenty
of steel-workers and foremen-fitters, dockers and printing
tradesmen who *could* afford Public School fees, if they chose to
spend their money that way, better than many gentlemen who
scrimp and save to send their sons and grandsons to Public
Schools. My own father was an impecunious Infantry Officer
and came of a line of the same breed; I know what he denied
himself, including for instance giving up his only Club, so that
I and my brothers could have the same sort of education that
his father (who incidentally was a country parson) had given
him—and he was no rare exception.

If there were anything in the theory that to abolish the Public
Schools would really improve British education as a whole by

releasing staff and accommodation for wider use, there might be a case for it; but there is not; it would merely eliminate something that is irreplaceable by other means—and the Country would be the poorer.

★   ★   ★

Haileybury is a school with a great tradition of service to India, having opened in 1852 as the East India Company's training college. In the years that followed a substantial proportion of its output went to the British and Indian Armies—its most famous soldier was Lord Allenby, after whom one of the Houses is now named. So perhaps it was natural that in the first Great War many old Haileyburians should have been attracted to the Air Service. We also sent a good many old boys to the Navy, when the Britannia and Osborne ceased to be the only avenue of entry to that Service, not long before the war—I believe I am right in saying that we can claim to have produced more Flag Officers than any other Public School.

One of the great architects of the R.A.F. was "Brookham"—Air Chief Marshal Sir Robert Brooke-Popham—the first Commandant of the R.A.F. Staff College. I remember him as a Major in the 52nd Light Infantry, seconded to the Royal Flying Corps, coming back to his old school in 1913 to give a lecture illustrated by lantern slides, one of which was a curious whirling disc which it was difficult to recognize as an aero-engine—the old Gnome rotary. Perhaps that lecture was responsible for quite a spate of O.H's going to the R.F.C. a year or two later. I have a photograph on my desk taken at an Air Staff conference at Old Sarum in 1948 of seven O.H's, which was rather a remarkable collection for one school and of whom five had been at Brookham's lecture thirty-five years before. In the centre is the then Prime Minister, Mr. Attlee, flanked by three Commanders-in-Chief, W. H. Dickson (Middle East), A. P. M. Sanders (British Air Forces in Germany), Brian Baker (Transport Command), the President of the Ordnance Board, G. A. H. Pidcock, the Commandant of the Imperial Defence

College, myself, and G. F. A. Day who won renown as the gallant Senior British Officer in Stalagluft III. All but the first and last had been boys at Haileybury together. And a couple of years later, under that same O.H. Prime Minister, we actually had a majority of O.H's on the Air Council—myself as C.A.S., Sanders as D.C.A.S., Dickson as A.M.S.O. and Geoffrey de Freitas, Parliamentary Under-Secretary.

Many others rose to high rank in the R.A.F.—including John Whitley the present Controller of the R.A.F. Benevolent Fund and Tom Prickett now commanding Air Support Command. I hope there will be many more in the years to come.

*   *   *

I think most normal boys are happy at their Public Schools—I know I was; there are always the odd misfits—often estimable characters—who are not, and they would be better off at a Day-school; but they are the exceptions—anyway they were in my day and I'm sure still are. Perhaps I was lucky; if anything the odds were slightly against my being able really to enjoy life at school. I was not of that rather rare intellectual type of boy who gets a tremendous kick out of book-learning as such; and being lame, could not play Rugger, the best of all games, and was at best a very indifferent cricketer. But I was able to make up for that in other ways. Thanks to the self-denying kindness of my father I was able to hunt a bit on a hireling with Mr. Smith-Bosanquet's Hounds. I had the odd day beating (for a shilling a day!) for Otto Beit's tremendous pheasant battues at Panshanger. There was a period when Frankie French (a distant cousin in the same House) and I kept —quite illegally—a couple of ferrets for rabbiting on Hertford Heath; I can't honestly say we killed many rabbits but we enjoyed ourselves, probably the more so because the ferrets' clandestine residence was in an unfrequented corner of a garden belonging to one of the Masters—a meek, unsuspicious and very raggable clergyman who taught, I think, Mathematics and Divinity. I played a bit of golf and, in Spring and Summer,

coxed a four on the Lea at Broxbourne. And in general I was
fortunate in being the sort of boy who was quite happy rather
aimlessly "mucking about" in the country—it was lovely
country round Haileybury and, I am glad to say, still is, though
so near London.

I was never a tiger for work though I did ultimately attain,
by pressure from below, to the Lower Sixth. But it is not only
or even especially in the class-room that many of the most
valuable lessons are to be learnt. I used to say at Camberley and
the Imperial Defence College that the chaps learnt more from
their fellow-students than from the Directing Staff; and up to a
point that is true of a Public School. Mixing as one did twenty-
four hours a day with a lot of other boys, surely taught us to
know *people*—to cultivate a sense of human values—and there
are few things more important than that in later life. One
learnt to distinguish the really good man from the flat-catcher;
discovered that intellectual brilliance or athletic eminence is not
everything—and conversely that the rather self-effacing intellectual or the not very clever Rugger "blood" could be a far
more valuable member of the community than sometimes
appeared on the surface; one learnt to appreciate gentle good
manners (I am thinking especially of Merivale, a charming and
very intelligent boy in my House, who died as a subaltern in
France a week after the Armistice), and to sum up the swash-
buckler for what he was worth.

At Haileybury before the Kaiser's war we had to learn to live
reasonably tough; we slept forty to fifty in a huge, rather cold
dormitory; the ablution system, though adequate, was anything but luxurious; and the sanitary arrangements would not
be tolerated in any self-respecting barracks to-day. Last—but
far from least—we were taught the meaning of discipline; from
prefects as well as Masters we learnt that it is

> "Safest, easiest and best,
> Expeditious, wise and best
> To obey your orders."[3]

[3] Ibid.

and part of that lesson was to be able to take punishment without resentment, even if one felt privately that it was unfair; they certainly "beat on us with rods, for the love they bore us"[4] and in my turn as a prefect I had to cane other boys; I am not conscious of having been degraded by the first or brutalized by the second—there is an unconscionable amount of rubbish talked about corporal punishment in schools.

The College servants had something to teach us—from two of them especially I learnt much that was later to be useful to me about the Private Soldier. Jim Jordan, the Lawrence House "Toby"[5] was a Regular Infantry Reservist, a cheerful, unruffled little man, without illusions, who went quietly and efficiently about his not very glamorous job every day in term-time, including Sundays, from early morning until dewy eve when he would walk stolidly off to the College Arms for his pint. The other was the College porter, an old 21st Lancer with a large Kitchener moustache and stiffly pompous gait, by the name of Blyth—the Guardian of the Gate. I was to meet his type again in the Army, all over the Empire—though I admit seldom anything quite as fruitily Edwardian. He was a proper old scoundrel, as I used often to tell him, but a great favourite of mine and I of his; he had a soft spot for sons of Regular officers and I think especially for me as a relative of an officer of his old regiment, Charlie Cotesworth[6] who was seventeen years a subaltern in the 21st. Blyth never tired in later years of telling—with many "Cors!" and chuckles—the story of my hi-jacking my father's charger to ride up from Broxbourne station to get Mr. Malim to sign my application for a Commission.[7] He was a great one for the gentle art of repartee. One day when he was collecting Lists at lunch in Hall, banter from the tables bouncing off him like peas off a drum, I complained loudly that I had found a dead caterpillar in my cabbage;

[4] Ibid.

[5] Servant, who cleaned the shoes and made the beds etc., for 40 or 50 boys.

[6] He with whom I used to stay and hunt in the "Ringwell" country in later years. See page 6.

[7] See *The Central Blue*, page 7.

"Oooh," he said in a hoarse and faintly beery whisper, "you'd better keep that dark, Sir, or we shall have all the young gentlemen wanting one." No one got much change out of old Bill Blyth.

*   *   *

The fact that to-day I could not translate a sentence of Cicero or a single stanza of Greek verse if my life depended on it, does not shake my conviction that the teaching at Haileybury was very good in my time—and I have no doubt still is. Mr. Toby Garland I shall always believe to have been one of the best Classics teachers that ever was; a tall, angular bachelor with a grey walrus moustache, he had a superficially intimidating manner accentuated by a rather harsh voice—I can still hear his "Brekekekex—Coax, Coax" when reading from *the Frogs* of Aristophanes. I remember my astonishment on first joining his Greek set at being actually *issued* with an excellent crib—the Loeb edition of Theocritus; he wanted us to appreciate Greek verse as living poetry about real everyday people in ancient Hellas, instead of being bored by it as just something over which one sweated one's guts out trying to cope with grammar and syntax.

From the Masters too we carried into later life more than just the facts of history and geography, the complexities of algebra (which were always beyond me) or the ability to construe Latin and Greek . . . The war soon drove all that out of our minds— though I still believe that a background of the Classics is of real value in any walk of life. My House Master in Lawrence House —so called after one of those great Haileyburians who were the founders of British India—was F. W. Headley, irreverently known as "Dog" Headley to many generations of boys. A small, wiry man with a tanned face and iron-grey beard, he was in his middle fifties when I joined—a prodigious age to a brat of 13—and had been a Master at Haileybury for over thirty years. A fine scholar (he had written books on abstruse subjects like Darwinism), he never had to put up with me in Form—he taught on the Modern Side—but I look back on him as a kind and understanding House Master. He had his mannerisms, as

2*

do so many elderly bachelor schoolmasters, one of which was to preface an opening remark with a mumbled "Ho, Ho". He was a great naturalist and bird-watcher—and incidentally a marvellous bird photographer, especially considering the rather primitive equipment of his day; and he would often take me and other boys on local expeditions—to hear the night-jar on the Heath ("Ho, Ho, come out and listen to the night-jar") or watch snipe and reed-warblers in the Lea marshes. I owe some of what I have of understanding of country things and my fondness for birds to old Dog Headley—and that surely is a good lasting gift to bequeath to any boy.

He was succeeded in my last term by L. A. Speakman, a very different type some twenty years younger—a lean, fit man, a bit prickly till one got to know him, and himself an old Haileyburian. Again, I was never in his Form—he was head of the Army Class—but I had a term as one of his prefects in Lawrence and he was very kind to me. He was a scratch golfer, in spite of having to wear thick spectacles, and took the trouble to try to improve my golf on that nice little course near Ware—his own lovely low rising drives and crisp deadly iron shots used to fill me with envious despair. "Speakers" remained a close friend of mine till his death in 1956.

These men in the days of Wynne-Wilson and Malim were very good, both as teachers and as men of original character and selfless devotion; I know their type still abounds in the Public Schools.

* * *

"Eheu fugaces, Postume, Postume, labuntur anni"—but I remember them all so vividly; L. S. Milford—"Po-face" from his bald head—an indefatigable recorder in the *Haileyburian* of O.H. doings, who tried to teach me Latin; Sam Toyne, the mighty rackets player who left us to be Head of St. Peter's, York; Jack Turner, quiet, wise and worldly; and old "Kib" Hoare who had initiated the School O.T.C. Camps in 1889 and got a C.B. in my first term—a rich vintage character if ever there was one. There was "Daddy" Wright, courtly and gentle, with his grey beard and stately walk, and Sunderland Lewis who tried to make a choir-boy of me—very raggable, with his lisp and quick temper. Three who were Masters in my day were destined to be killed in action—George Waters, House Master of Trevelyan, in France, C. J. Reid and G. E. Grundy with the same battalion on Gallipoli. Dear George Grundy—I had a couple of terms in his Form and we were very fond of him, with his nervous habit of slapping the back of his neck when irritated almost beyond endurance by our stupidity; he also was eminently raggable, almost too easy a subject for so skilled an exponent of that subtle and delicate art as A. B. Wright[8]—though I do recall one occasion when A.B. *just* over-played his hand and was bitten with sudden and surprising ferocity by our usually tolerant Form Master.

Others whom I looked upon as special friends were dapper little Mr. Kennedy, a reputedly rich bachelor who used to hunt, and keep an eye on me out hunting to see I did not do anything too silly; and Jerome Farrell, later Director of Education in Palestine. Farrell, also a bachelor and believed to be well off, always dressed in a rather unorthodox way for a schoolmaster —good tweed suits, and shoes gleaming like old mahogany. He was a bit unorthodox in other ways—he would have a few of the older boys in for coffee, and even the occasional glass of sherry, in his rooms in Clock House which were beautifully furnished, with good Medici prints on the walls; and he went out of his way to instil in me some appreciation of Italian Renaissance art and the quality of men like Michelangelo and Leonardo da Vinci.

* * *

One could go on and on—but enough! And now, of course, they are all gone. "Men of little showing" maybe—but famous men for all that. May they rest in peace. I and quite a lot of other old gentlemen still living owe them a debt we could never repay.

[8] In later years, Sir Andrew Wright, K.C.M.G., C.B.E., M.C., Governor of Cyprus.

3   Eastern Adventure: The Middle East and the Sudan, 1915–1916

The issue of "helmets tropical" to the two Squadrons of Lieut-Colonel Geoffrey Salmond's 5th Wing Royal Flying Corps in the autumn of 1915 sent a buzz of excited speculation and unfounded rumour round the Messes and barrack rooms of the old Fort Grange at Gosport.

I rather fancied myself in my "helmet tropical". It was less than six months since my unorthodox entry into the Air Service and I still had only about 60 hours solo flying in my log book; but I had crammed a good deal into that short period. I had broken one or two old Longhorns[1] learning to fly at Brooklands—where on one occasion an engine failure taking off had involved me in an insalubriously close acquaintanceship with the famous sewage farm. I had delivered a new B.E.2.C—a fabulously modern and powerful machine with a 90 h.p. engine —from the works at Coventry to Major Newall's[2] Squadron at St. Omer during the battle of Loos, and had made a vain attempt to persuade him to keep me in France. I had got away with a rather alarming little crash in Thames fog on descending after a very amateur and wholly ineffectual encounter with a Zeppelin in the dark over London. And here I was now, at an age when but for the Kaiser I should still have been at Haileybury, trying on a new headgear of a kind with which I was familiar from photographs of my father on a pony against the background of an old thatched bungalow in Bareilly when I was a baby.

*   *   *

[1] The Maurice Farman pusher biplane with an elevator in front.
[2] The late Marshal of the R.A.F., Lord Newall.

My heart swelled with pride. But what did it mean? Where were we going? Gallipoli? "Mespot"? Egypt? No one knew, though some pretended to. Anyway it clearly was not the Western Front—to the undisguised relief of my mother during my short embarkation leave at home.

My soldier-servant, an old 16th Lancer generally known as "Trooper" Savage—a vintage character with an absolutely expressionless face and a bow-legged, slightly swaggering horseman's gait—knew it was India. I did not fancy that somehow. Rupert Brooke had been dead some months, and it would be misleading to suggest that his spirit of dedicated adventure still burned very bright in that autumn of Neuve Chapelle and Suvla Bay. But there were some of us who very privately still thanked God for having matched us with His hour—and India seemed very far away from the war.

I need not have worried. Trooper Savage did not. Having served in India and Egypt before the war, he was up to the tricks of them niggers and was able, while brushing my uniforms, to impart to me in an impassive monotone select titbits of information about them—in the intervals of hissing gently as if he were strapping a horse. One bright October morning we were off, marching to entrain at Fort Rowner, the domed "helmets tropical" looking strangely incongruous above the serge maternity jackets—the high-collared, double-breasted tunic of the R.F.C. And at sunset we were leaning on the rail of the troopship *Scotian* out of Avonmouth, watching the coast of Somerset slide by in the gathering darkness, having learnt that our destination was Gallipoli.

* * *

We were too late. The echoes of our anchor cable had barely died away around the crowded roadstead of Mudros, the base for the Gallipoli campaign, when a destroyer came in at speed bearing no less a person than Lord Kitchener, come to discuss with the Commander-in-Chief the evacuation of the Peninsula. I always suspect, looking back on it, that—the original reason

for our presence in the Eastern theatre of war having evaporated
—G.H.Q. perhaps understandably did not know what on earth
to do with us. Anyway there was a marked absence of urgency
about the subsequent proceedings as far as we were concerned.
We hung about in Mudros harbour for a week or so waiting to
hear our fate. We went for rather disconsolate walks on the
dusty, dirty island of Lemnos among the base depots, dumps,
mule lines, field hospitals and Australian rest-camps with their
stinking incinerators. We exchanged courtesies with the officers
of the Russian Cruiser *Askold*—known to the troops as "the
packet of Woodbines" from her row of five or six thin funnels;
the Czar's Navy was dry for the duration and the poor chaps
more than made up for it when they visited us aboard *Scotian*.
And at last we left in a quite unwarrantable hurry for Egypt;
Jock Will[3] and I were ashore stretching our legs and arrived
back at the jetty to see *Scotian* making for the harbour mouth—
a predicament from which we were rescued by a kindly naval
officer with a picket boat.

Arrived in Egypt, no-one seemed to be in any hurry to get us
into battle. 14 Squadron went off to the Western Desert, but we
of No. 17 were dumped into a base camp at Alexandria where
I enjoyed my first experience of shooting duck and snipe in the
shallows of Lake Mariut, and fell in love with a classically
beautiful Greek girl in Mr. Groppi's shop. Then we were
moved to Heliopolis to connect with our aircraft which we
erected and fitted with guns and bomb-sights, and did a bit of
training. We enjoyed ourselves in Cairo; saw the sights and
smelled the smells; drank a weird and wonderful cocktail—
three or four distinct layers of different coloured alcohol—in
Gasparini's bar; sat on the terrace of Shepheard's and listened to
relays of thirsty Australians assuring us that they had been the
last man to leave the Gallipoli Peninsula; drove the electric
trams furiously in and out between Heliopolis and Cairo, to the
helpless indignation of the Egyptian drivers and the understandable concern of the civilian passengers—and generally

[3] A famous Scottish Rugger cap before the war.

behaved or misbehaved ourselves as young officers are liable to do when they have nothing better to keep them out of mischief. My Uncle William Hayter, then legal adviser to the Egyptian Government, lived on Gezireh island, where I was hospitably entertained in a house internally indistinguishable from any English home in Hampshire, and played with my small cousin Priscilla.[4] It was all very pleasant but much too leisurely and unwarlike, and I was not the only one of us who felt it was hardly what we had joined the Army to do.

★   ★   ★

However, at last this came to an end. 30 Squadron had left the Suez Canal for Mesopotamia, and 17 was sent to replace them; so early in February C Flight found itself under canvas on an aerodrome consisting of a flattish bit of dun waste of which the boundaries were marked by whitewashed oil-drums, alongside the base depot north of Suez where the air was filled with the sound of camels bubbling and snarling and the smell of dust and incinerators. But at last there was something to do that bore some resemblance to war though, it must be confessed, one had to look pretty hard for it. It was about a year since the only serious Turkish attempt on the Canal had been repulsed. But another attack in force was still thought possible after the evacuation of Gallipoli, and actually we now know that the Turks were in fact contemplating something on quite a big scale. But it never got beyond the stage of contemplation. In the words of the Official History—"reconnaissances by the Royal Flying Corps and the seaplanes of the R.N.A.S. established the fact that there were no considerable Turkish forces in Sinai and no signs of a concentration in Southern Palestine for an attack on Egypt".

So that is what we were doing—establishing the fact that there was nothing very much for us to do, anyway in our Southern sector of the Eastern Desert though farther north

---

[4] Priscilla Napier, the authoress of *A Late Beginner* (Michael Joseph, London), a very entertaining account of a childhood in Cairo in those days.

there were a number of minor actions between British Yeo-
manry and small detachments of Turks, or of Bedouin under
Turkish officers, and one or two more serious actions such as
those at Qatiya and Romani. We patrolled the waterless desert
east of the Canal and the passes through the Sinai hills,[5] shooting up the odd enemy patrol and bombing their few small posts
near water-holes like Ain Sudr and Moiya Harab; photo-
graphed and occasionally bombed more important road centres
like Kossaima and El Hassana and the little town of Nekhl—
including on one occasion when Enver Pasha was supposed to
be inspecting the garrison—and generally did our best to justify
our existence. We bathed in the Canal and ate enormous
prawns in the little restaurant overlooking the Red Sea at Port
Tewfik (I sometimes wondered what diet it was that made
those prawns so fat!); and we got rather restive—I don't think
any of us felt we were doing anything of much importance.

*   *   *

So it was with real excitement that we heard, about the middle
of April, that we were to pack up and go off to some little
campaign that was due to start in the Sudan. We hoped that at
last there would be something worthwhile for us to do, and
anyway it was a thrill to think that we were to fly the first aeroplanes ever to appear somewhere in the middle of darkest
Africa—a place called Darfur that none of us had ever heard of.
We were told the Sultan of Darfur had been something to do
with the Khalifa; and I saw visions of Dervishes attacking
zarebas, the 21st Lancers charging at Omdurman (illustrations
by R. Caton Woodville) and even of myself in a tarbush like
that in the photograph of my Uncle Herbert during his Egyptian Army days in the River Campaign. As a matter of fact some
of these visions were to materialize (not the tarbush) though in
a form rather different to what I had anticipated, and were to
include the first occasion on which I took part in what (with a

---

[5] An area where the place-names brought back many memories to me in
the six-day war of 1967.

bit of artistic licence) might be described as a battle. I am bound
to confess that the Official History describes it rather slightingly
as an Affair—"the Affair of Beringia". I have a feeling that the
Dervishes, who suffered very heavy casualties (over 1,000 out
of a force of about 8,000), would have called it something more
dignified. Anyway as far as I was concerned it was a Battle, and
what is more I got myself wounded in it—one of the only two
officer casualties in that great campaign—and so later was able
to wear the thin strip of gold braid called a "wound-stripe",
worn on the sleeve of the khaki tunic, that was one of the
sartorial peculiarities of the 1914–18 war.

Perhaps I should just outline the earlier course of what the
Official History[6] describes as "a campaign remarkable for the
distances covered in waterless country and for the revival of the
old Dervish tactics of attempting to rush a square". The Sultan
Ali Dinar, who as one of the Khalifa's Emirs had been involved
in that affair with the 21st Lancers at Omdurman, was being
egged on by the Germans and Turks to make a nuisance of himself in conjunction with the Senussi activities in the North, with
the object of containing British troops away from more important fronts. Eventually it was decided to deal with him and take
over the old kingdom of Darfur as a province of the Anglo-
Egyptian Sudan. For this purpose the Sirdar, Sir Reginald
Wingate (who had been Kitchener's Chief of Staff in the River
War of 1896–97), concentrated near the Kordofan-Darfur
border, under Colonel Kelly of the 3rd Hussars, a nice old-
fashioned little force called the Western Frontier Force—two
Companies Mounted Infantry, six 12½-pounder mountain guns,
a Maxim battery, five Companies Camel Corps, six Sudanese,
two Arab and three Egyptian infantry companies—to which
were added at the end of April two aeroplanes of 17 Squadron.
After seizing the first well-centre across the border at Gebel
Hilla, which they had done in March, the Force had a distance
of some 170 miles to go, via two other water-points at Abiad
Wells and Meleit, to reach Ali Dinar's capital at El Fasher. The

6 *Military Operations, Egypt and Palestine.* H.M.S.O., 1928.

capital was a fair-sized town of about 50,000 inhabitants, mostly straw *tukls*[7] but with a few more pretentious whitewashed mud houses, including Ali Dinar's palace; otherwise the villages were small clusters of *tukls* round a well, or more often depending for their existence on water stored during the rains in the hollow trunks of the great *tebeldi* trees that dotted the landscape, sticking up all over the dun waste of sand and thorn scrub that is Darfur in summer. Ali Dinar's Dervish Army comprised about 5,000 riflemen, 1,000 Baggara and Rizighat horsemen and numerous assorted tribesmen armed with swords or broad-bladed spears.

★   ★   ★

There were certain difficulties about aviation in Darfur in 1916. Maps for instance; we were issued with things like large coarse handkerchiefs—and mainly as blank as a handkerchief. The well-centres were marked, not very accurately, and there would be a splendid looking road marked by a red line— splendid looking until one looked more closely and found that "this track was reported to be here by a trader in 1883". There were, of course, no real roads. It was some 300 miles to our base at Gebel Hilla from the railhead, where we erected our aeroplanes which had been shipped from Suez to Port Sudan and thence on by train; and to make it easier for us to find our way the W.F.F. had thoughtfully pegged out large arrows of white calico at intervals of about 10 miles along their track. Actually this turned out not to be quite such a good idea as it might have been because the local Kordofani couturiers thought they were just the job for this year's spring models for the girls. I had a forced landing at a village called Abu Zabbad, about 100 miles on the way to Gebel Hilla when my nose was bleeding freely and I thought I was going to faint (which actually I have never done in my life); I had not seen many arrows on the way; but, though most of the ladies of Abu Zabbad wore practically nothing, I saw one or two wearing very natty white

---

[7] Round conical huts built with the stalks of *dhurra,* the local grain.

mini-skirts. So, as a navigational aid, white calico had its limit-
ations.

*　　*　　*

The advance on El Fasher began early in May. One of the first
things we had to do was to drop warning notices calling on the
enemy to surrender, and warning the civil population to keep
away from the area of operations in case they got hurt; I think
this was probably the first occasion on which the warning
notice from the air was used, though of course it became regular
practice in tribal operations in later years. Ali Dinar merely
replied by sending rude messages to the Sirdar; so Kelly said—
like Sam Small's old Duke of Wellington—"Let battle com-
mence", and on May 15th the Western Frontier Force, which
had previously concentrated forward at Abiad Wells, moved
out on their 120-mile march to El Fasher.

The column advanced in the traditional square formation
with the transport, field hospital, guns, etc. in the centre. At the
end of the day's march they halted and bivouacked in the same
formation, a *zareba* of thorn bushes with the business ends out-
wards was cut and laid, shallow shelter trenches dug and sentry
groups posted. They advanced at a rate of about 20 miles a day,
and the whole thing was worked out to a time programme.
Very little enemy opposition was encountered. The duty of the
aeroplanes during the advance was to reconnoitre ahead of the
column, to keep any villages or well-centres under observation,
to clear out the enemy detachments by direct action with the
bomb and Lewis gun where necessary, and finally to prospect
for water. Information was dropped by message bag—we had
no wireless equipment in the aircraft. We flew without obser-
vers, the second seat being occupied by an improvised extra
petrol tank to give us the necessary range.

The first point where any serious opposition was anticipated
was Meleit, a large well-centre and the last on the line to El
Fasher. On the 17th the two portions of the Force, the mounted
troops and the slow moving infantry and transport which had
been divided during the interim period for watering purposes

between Hilla and Abiad, joined up at a pre-arranged concentration point under the Gebel Hebella about one day's march short of Meleit. On the same day my Flight Commander, Captain Bannatyne, flying low over Meleit, was fired on from the villages; an enemy force estimated at about 500 was holding the wells and Bannatyne attacked them with bombs and Lewis gun fire, whereupon they cleared out. On the following morning I was over Meleit just before and during the time that the Force entered it; the only sign of the enemy was an occasional horseman mounting hurriedly and galloping away towards El Fasher, and the Force occupied the villages without a shot being fired.

A three days' halt was made at Meleit to rest and water men and animals; during this period several reconnaissances were flown and the enemy were reported in force north of El Fasher. But the weather was now beginning to break and the air was always full of drifting dust which made it extremely difficult to make out anything on the ground. Indeed, throughout the 21st and the 22nd the dust was blowing so hard that it was practically impossible to do anything; in addition a shower of rain fell on the 21st, with the result that there was a thick haze on the 22nd. Bannatyne and another pilot called Bellamy (there were only the three of us) both went out on that day but were unable to see anything; one of them actually passed over the column without being able to see it. The Force was timed to leave Meleit at dawn on the 22nd and it was anticipated that the enemy would stand and fight somewhere on that day, which in fact he did; but the weather was against us and the aeroplanes could take no part in the day's fighting.

*   *   *

What had actually happened was this: the Force left at 5.30 a.m. on the 22nd and immediately met with much more serious opposition from horsemen and camelry than had previously been encountered. It was several times necessary to halt and bring the screw-guns into action to disperse the large numbers of mounted men that gathered on the flanks, and at about eleven o'clock the main body of the enemy was sighted holding a strong position on high ground south of the village of Beringia. Colonel Kelly, knowing the temperament of the Dervish, halted the square and sent a company of Camel Corps forward towards the enemy position. This soon had the desired effect of drawing the enemy out of his position, and about noon the whole Dervish army advanced in mass and made a desperate attack on the square. The assault was carried out with great gallantry, but they had not a chance in that mass formation against the Maxim guns and rifles from the square; and after being in action about half an hour they broke and ran, hotly pursued by our counter-attack. Their losses in this fight were about 1,000, and there were dead Dervishes riddled with bullets lying within ten yards of the guns. The force then advanced and went into *zareba* for the night a few miles north of the town.

★   ★   ★

That dust storm and the rain that followed it on the 21st gave us at Gebel Hilla some rather uneasy moments. We had no communication with the column, but knew they must be within striking distance of El Fasher where it seemed certain Ali Dinar would put up a fight. So the vile visibility on the 22nd, coupled with the very inadequate maps and primitive navigational methods of those days, resulting in two pilots in succession being unable to find the Force, was a bit of a worry. The weather was a nuisance not only to the pilots but to the airmen—the indefatigable Sergeant Hemming and his henchmen Parfitt and Johnson, White and Clark. It was no mean job keeping engines and Lewis guns in working condition with the air permanently thick with drifting sand, and having to work long hours in canvas tent-hangars in which the temperature was always well into the hundreds. But they did a herculean job and we never had an engine failure—though the old Lewis guns did let us down occasionally.

By the way, those little tent-hangars, every drop of petrol

and a spare engine all did the 300 miles up from railhead on the backs of camels, which I'm afraid resulted in a pretty high death-rate among the poor beasts and, incidentally, something like a 50 per cent rate of evaporation from the standard two-gallon petrol cans.

It may be imagined that it was a slightly anxious little knot of chaps who saw me off from Gebel Hilla when my turn came to take off before dawn on the 23rd, to find the lost column and take part in the battle which we all hoped would be taking place before El Fasher. I can still remember being rather un-enthusiastic about sweet tea and fried eggs at four o'clock in the morning—I have never been at my best at that hour, whether the occasion was some martial exercise or merely pulling on cold boots to go cubbing in a peaceful English September dawn. It is all right when one is actually in the air or on the back of a horse hacking off to meet hounds, but the preliminaries—let's face it—are cheerless. Anyway, by about five o'clock that morning I was airborne under the vast African sky ablaze with stars, the red glow from the exhausts punctuated by the occa-sional mauve flash as the engine warmed up, and the moonlight reflected on the tin top-cowling and rows of dancing tappets. Soon after getting set on my compass bearing, with the aid of a little electric torch, the lovely flush of dawn began to appear in the East and before long the sun was pushing up over the hills behind me, bathing the aeroplane in a soft glow—the air-screw a shimmering, translucent disc of golden light in front. The sky was flecked with little flamingo-pink clouds, while the earth below was still in hazy twilight—very hazy, because that dust was still drifting and visibility below the dust level was virtually nil.

However, the broad track made by the Force in its advance through the scrub was just distinguishable and in due course I found myself over the town of El Fasher. The populace were streaming out of the town with their flocks of goats and a few camels. To begin with I could see no signs either of the enemy or of our own Force, but as I passed low over the town for the

second time I was fired at by a motley crowd of horse and
camel men in the broad clearing in front of the Mosque. That
perhaps may have resulted from an Egyptian officer having
deserted to the enemy and revealed to them that we had been
briefed not to bomb in the vicinity of Mosques—an order on
which I'm afraid I turned a blind eye and let them have a drum
of Lewis gun and one of my four little 20-pound Hales bombs.
And then suddenly I saw away to the northward the flashes of
bursting shells through the haze—and there was my Battle, or
anyway the tail end of it.

I remember passing over a lot of rather spectacular warriors
on horses galloping southwards (i.e. away from the Force)
apparently in rather a hurry—some of them fired at me with
rifles held in one hand as they galloped. I took a chukker round
over the Force, who seemed to be quite all right, advancing
steadily in their usual square formation; so I turned back over
the retreating Baggara horsemen and gave them a drum of
Lewis gun and one bomb to speed the parting guests, and flew
on over El Fasher, to see if I could find something interesting to
tell Colonel Kelly, and incidentally a more rewarding target for
my two remaining bombs. I found it. Just south of the town
was the Dervish army, in a state of considerable disorder, to put
it mildly. I suppose there were about a couple of thousand of
them, horse and foot and some camelmen, milling around two
or three sort of focal points where the crowd was thickest. We
had been briefed that Ali Dinar himself had a very big white
Bishareen camel and a couple of outsize banners, and there in
the middle of one of the denser points in the crowd—rather like
that round the tote at a race-meeting—was a huge banner.
That, I thought, was the obvious target for my two little 20-
pound Hales and I duly let them go—unfortunately the drum I
had emptied at the Baggara horsemen had jammed on the
pillar, no doubt due to the drifting sand, and I had been unable
to replace it with a full one. Actually I had bad luck and can not
claim to have bagged Ali Dinar (he was eventually caught and
killed in a fight with a little force under Major Huddleston,

later Sirdar and then Governor of Chelsea Hospital, about the beginning of November). It would perhaps be more accurate to say that Ali Dinar had astonishingly good luck; he was on his camel, and we heard later than one of my bombs burst almost underneath the poor animal, blowing it to bits and killing a lot of men all round it, but the Sultan got away with a nasty headache.

Well . . . that was that; I had nothing left with which to make a nuisance of myself to the enemy—that empty ammunition drum was stuck to the Lewis gun as though it was riveted on. So I thought I'd better go and tell Force H.Q. what was happening—and at that moment I was hit. I was flying at about five or six hundred feet and a large, rather blunt lead bullet (which I have on a little mahogany mount on my desk as I write) came up through a packet of papers on the floor of my cockpit—mail which I was carrying to drop on Force H.Q.— and embedded itself in the fleshy part of my thigh. I bled like a pig all over Colonel Kelly's official mail and for the next few minutes was busy tying a First Field Dressing tightly round my right leg just below the groin to stop the bleeding. I then found myself in a bit of a quandary. The wounded leg did not hurt much—just felt numb—but it soon began to get stiff and I could not apply right rudder, which one did by pushing the right end of the rudder-bar forward. My left leg being normally the least serviceable of the two, I could not apply right rudder by pulling the left end of the rudder bar towards me by the toe-strap (it did occur to me later that the irate President of that War Office Medical Board about a year before might have had a quiet laugh if he had known what was happening). But I found I could just reach with my right hand over the side the cable connecting the rudder bar with the starboard pylon of the rudder, and could thus do what I could no longer do with my leg. That was all right as far as it went—unorthodox and uncomfortable, but effective. But, with one hand on the control column and the other on the rudder cable, in very turbulent air, I had no hands to spare with which to write a report of what had happened, stuff it in the message bag with the red, blue and yellow streamers and drop it on Force H.Q. I considered trying to land in the scrub alongside the column but decided there was not much future in that. I didn't much fancy the prospect of the long flight back to Gebel Hilla in those conditions—so, after orbiting over the column (who must have been wondering what the devil I thought I was doing) in an agony of indecision for about five minutes, I came to the rather craven conclusion that my best course was to beat it for Abiad Wells, which was not so far to go.

*   *   *

Thus I can not claim that my role in "The Affair of Beringia" was a very distinguished one. Actually I don't think it would have made the least difference if I had never been there. The Dervish army was already beaten, and the fact that I killed a few more of them and gave Ali Dinar a nasty jolt did not really affect the situation; and the one thing that Colonel Kelly really wanted of me (apart from his mail), namely a reconnaissance report on the situation in El Fasher and points south, I was unable to give him.

In due course I got back to Abiad and landed after 5½ hours in the air, and there then ensued a painful but in retrospect amusing surgical interlude. There was only one Field Hospital in the Western Frontier Force and that, at the moment, was just about entering El Fasher. But at Abiad was an Egyptian army doctor with a first aid kit, and it was decided (I think now probably quite unnecessarily) that the bullet should be extracted from my thigh at once. The first aid kit did not run to any anaesthetic but it did include (of all things) a couple of half bottles of very warm champagne. Moreover, the O.C. troops at Abiad was one Bimbashi Mills of the Eastern Arab Corps, a kindly but strong-minded officer, naturally much senior to me; and he had brought with him from Khartoum a couple of long boxes from Mr. Angelo Capato's store containing little somethings to eat and smoke and drink, wherewith to soften the rigours of the campaign; and they included a bottle of brandy. Bannatyne had flown up from Gebel Hilla, and he and Mills between them decided that as I could not be afforded the comfort of anaesthesia they would make me as drunk as they could before facing the operating table—in this case a native string bed in Mills's *tukl*.

Well, that was all right by me, though I date my lack of enthusiasm for champagne from that occasion. Before long, the two half-bottles plus a long pull at Mills's brandy—on top, I suppose, of a natural nervous reaction after rather an exciting morning—had done their work and I would cheerfully have faced a Caesarian operation if I had been told to, though I confess that somewhere beneath the pearly mists of inebriation there lurked a little black imp of lucidity warning me that this was not really going to be very funny. In due course I found myself, minus my trousers, lying face down on the string bed with Mills's heavy hand firmly on the small of my back, and the Egyptian doctor got to work. After the usual sinister preliminaries with iodine he plunged a knife into the back of my thigh, wobbled it about a bit and then pulled it out and squeezed. I squeaked and took a bite out of Mills's pillow, and the doctor had another go with his knife, squeezed again—and out popped the bullet.

A little over five weeks later I was landed at Southampton as a cot-case in the hospital ship *Delta*, just in time to hear of the great British offensive on the Somme which had opened that morning—1 July 1916. The news made my little adventures in Sinai and the Sudan seem pretty small potatoes.

4 Wings and Guns: The Western Front, 1917–1918

Someone once described war as months of boredom punctuated by moments of intense fear. Not a bad description—and in Hitler's war it was true, not only for the fighting men, but also for many civilian inhabitants of our cities. Was there not Mrs. Mop in the War Office—one of that indomitable tribe who, week after weary week, struggled daily to work through shattered streets in the Blitz—who, asked for news of her husband, replied, "He's in the Middle East—the bloody coward!"

I had my moments of intense fear like anyone else; but to be honest do not remember often being bored in war. In 1914–18 I was too young and in 1939–45 usually too busy to be bored much. In what was known for twenty years as "the Great War", we in the Royal Flying Corps were especially lucky in that respect. We always had the interest of "mucking about with aeroplanes", and the new thrill of flying. And we did not have to put up with the interminable hardship and squalor of life in the trenches—to say nothing of its dangers which, in the general run of things, were far more daunting than anything we had to endure. Not for us the weeks of existence in the presence of death, cooped up in a muddy, stinking ditch, sleeping in wet clothes in a foetid dug-out, plodding weary miles at night on ration fatigue over slimy duck-boards, patrols and wire-mending in no-man's-land under the cold rain of a Flemish winter—freezing face downwards in the mud when the German Verey light soared skyward. To us, seeing much of them as we did—though mostly when they were out of the Line in rest or reserve—without having to share their perils and discomforts, the courage and patient endurance of the Infantry in the first Great War was and is a source of never-ending admiration. I am not sure the Field Gunners didn't have a worse time than the Infantry in some ways. The battalions did get back out of range of shell and mortar fairly regularly on relief; but too often, anyway in 1917, the Infantry of a Division would be relieved and the Artillery left in position to cover the relieving troops. We airmen did at least live out of gun-range. We had relatively comfortable quarters—Nissen or Armstrong huts on the edge of some Picardy cow-pasture behind the balloon line where we could enjoy reasonably restful nights, to the accompaniment of the endless thump and grumble of artillery, with gun flashes and Verey lights flickering from dusk to dawn like summer lightning on the Eastern horizon.

*   *   *

The spring and early summer of 1917 was a critical time for the Royal Flying Corps on the Western Front. The German Air Service had taken a heavy knock during the Somme battles of the previous summer, when our air superiority had been almost complete. But that was followed in the autumn by Von Hoeppner's reorganization and the appearance of the new Albatross, Fokker and Halberstadt fighters—and a rather formidable two-seater called the Hanoveranner; while our own fighter—or "scout" squadrons as they were quaintly called (the last thing they did was scouting)—in the spring of '17 were still in the early stages of re-equipping with the S.E. 5 and Camel and our own good two-seater, the Bristol Fighter. The early spring battles had, therefore, seen very heavy losses in the R.F.C.; so much so that No. 58 Squadron, which had been forming to come out as reinforcement, was broken up to find drafts to replace casualties in France, and I found myself posted as a Flight Commander to No. 5 Squadron on the First Army front near Arras—they were called "Corps Squadrons" in those days because they were allotted on the basis of one to each Army Corps in the Line.

That spring and summer was the hey-day of Von Richt-

ofen's famous "circus"—the big formations of red fighters that
wrought considerable havoc at that time, especially among the
Corps Squadrons whose B.E.2.E and R.E.8 two-seaters were
pretty easy meat for fast single-seaters. Painting them bright
red was a psychologically clever move, its reasons—or so I have
always imagined—being much the same as those for the war-
paint of the old American Indians and some other savage tribes.
It certainly had a marked moral effect on some people—including myself. Richtofen and his "Red Devils" were boosted by
the popular Press at home (rather as Rommel was a quarter of a
century later); aircrew back from a tour of operations for a
spell as instructors in England "shot their lines" as returned
warriors are liable to do; and the new boy just out from home
meeting a red-painted enemy tended to jump to the conclusion
that here was the redoubtable Richtofen in person. But apart
from that, the Circus was really very good—far better than the
average run of German fighters who, fortunately, usually
lacked that flat-out offensive spirit which Trenchard inspired in
all the Squadrons under his command. It was the exception to
see German fighters our side of the Line, whereas our offensive
patrols always operated deep into enemy territory.

*   *   *

The job of the Corps Squadrons was close co-operation with
the Army, or rather with the troops on the ground—we were
all in the Army in those days. The bulk of the work was observation for the artillery, the huge masses of guns and howitzers
of all calibres from 13 pounder to 15 inch—sometimes during
an attack almost wheel to wheel—that were such a feature of
the Western front from 1915 to 1918. This consisted of counter-
battery work—destroying or neutralizing enemy artillery—and
trench work, destroying enemy trenches and cutting wire.
And, since the former predominated, two of the three Flights
(each of six aircraft) in the Corps Squadron were usually
Counter-battery Flights and the third a Trench Flight, which
also had the rather unenviable job in an offensive of what was

called Contact Patrol—reporting the progress of the attacking infantry who notified their position by lighting special flares as they reached their successive objectives. Actually this form of specialization was not always adhered to—the organization had to be flexible—but there was a good deal to be said for it; it did mean that after some months on the same sector of the front one got to know the Counter-battery area or the trench system like the back of one's hand. Thus, though I never did a Contact Patrol—being a Counter-battery Flight Commander—I did do a good deal of trench bombardment and wire-cutting; but I never got to know the German trench-system as intimately as I did the Counter-battery area where every enemy battery position was, so to speak, an old friend and any new construction, changed position or fresh track was instantly obvious. Every gun-pit and yard of trench was shown exactly on the maps which were made from and kept up-to-date by the air photography that was also the job of the Corps Squadrons.

As a relaxation from these routine but seldom uninteresting activities we indulged, on moonlight nights, in some rather aimless bombing and machine-gunning of billeting zones, approach roads, aerodromes and so on in the enemy back areas. It was a quite enjoyable but I don't think really very useful exercise—though I admit that on the comparatively rare occasions when the Germans bombed our back areas we did not like it very much; so maybe it had some moral effect in giving the enemy soldier the feeling that, even when he was out of the Line, he was not secure from the death that flieth by night.

★   ★   ★

Anywhere in the vicinity of the front line itself the whole country looked from the air rather like a vast plate of dirty porridge—one churned mass of overlapping shell holes, water in the bottoms reflecting the sky—the tracery of the forward trench systems and the grey or rusty brown of the wire running through it, often almost obliterated in some places. Further back in the enemy artillery area the country, peppered with

battery positions and criss-crossed with support and communication trenches, was not quite so pitted with shell holes except
in the immediate vicinity of the batteries. The villages were
piles of shattered rubble and the woods dreary cemeteries of
dead trees lifting gaunt branches and broken trunks to the sky;
but there were green patches of untended grass or root-crops,
and here and there a drift of scarlet where the poppies had
spread over the untilled land. Beyond that again on our Corps
front the elaborate pattern of chalk parapets that was the
Queant-Drocourt switch, a northward extension of the Hin-
denburg line, looked like a long white lace scarf thrown across
the unscarred fields.

I was to drive through that same country twenty-three years
later during the crisis of the Battle of France, and all those
names came back to me with such vivid clarity—those places
that I knew so well in the summer following the capture of the
Vimy Ridge; Arleux and Neuvireil, Fresnoy and Gavrelle,
Oppy Wood and Square Wood and the Bois du T.

Every enemy battery had its allotted code number and every
bit of trench its name, Link Maze, Crumpet trench, Lambert
Alley and so on. The fall of shell was reported by clock-code
with lettered concentric circles giving distance and the clock
numbers the bearing from the ranging point. Our means of
communication was Morse on a rather primitive wireless set,
air to ground only; the gunners could communicate with us
only by means of white oil-cloth strips laid out on the ground.
But both partners got pretty expert at it; after I'd been doing it
for a few months I prided myself on being able to range two
and sometimes even three batteries on different targets at the
same time—it was only a question of being reasonably quick at
Morse, timing one's calls for fire right, and being in the right
position to see the right target at the right moment. But it did
call for some concentration and, largely for that reason, the job
of the observer, with his one or two Lewis guns in a rotating
Scarff ring behind the pilot, became almost exclusively that of
what would now be called a tail gunner. There was no better

way of qualifying for a place in one of those beautifully kept Imperial War Graves gardens that dot the plains of Belgium and Northern France to-day than for both men in an old R.E.8 to have their eyes on the ground. So the pilot flew the aeroplane (which, of course, became almost instinctive and called for hardly a thought) and did the job, tapping the little Morse key under his right hand, and was able to give his whole attention to the ground, confident that his observer was watching the sky above and behind him ready to warn him if enemy fighters came unpleasantly close.

★   ★   ★

One had the occasional home leave, the joy of climbing into the crowded leave-train at rail-head and seeing again that very horsey-looking Military Landing Officer with the khaki hunting-tie at Boulogne—or was it Calais? But apart from that and the occasional interruptions by bad weather, day after day for nearly a year I ranged batteries of all shapes and sizes— 6 inch, 8 inch and 9.2 inch howitzers, the long 6 inch Mark VII guns and, occasionally as a treat, the huge 15 inch howitzers of the Royal Marine Artillery—the Blue Marines whom I had known so well at Eastney Barracks in my boyhood days before the war. The crossed cannon above the Royal Marine cap-badge brought back nostalgic memories of Eastney—the R.M.A. swagger-stick that had been a small boy's pride and joy, the thrill of bugles in the early morning, the old wooden "beehive" garrison Church on Sundays with the band of the School of Music instead of an organ, and the gleam of silver on that Mess table where, as a subaltern at Gosport, I had my first experience of getting rather tight on a guest-night with my Uncle Herbert in 1915. That old 15 inch monster really was a pleasure to observe for—the first round perhaps 300 yards over, the second 200 yards short and the third, as often as not, bang on the target. Its shells were colossal; the explosion covered about an acre; and sometimes one could see the round passing at the top of its trajectory, bumbling along quite slowly and looking like a locomotive boiler on the loose.

I suppose to some that will be a new idea—that one can see shells in flight. Actually you can see them for a second or two after leaving the guns if you stand close behind the battery; but at the height at which we in the Corps Squadrons used to fly they were a familiar sight and, I think, accounted for not a few of our casualties. The anti-aircraft fire of those days was unpleasant but not very lethal, unless one made a habit of flying for too long on a dead-straight course and at constant speed and height; "Archie" it was called in 1914–18—in those days no-one had heard of "flak". There was also a curious form of incendiary anti-aircraft missile, known as a Flaming Onion which actually it did resemble—if anyone has seen an onion on fire! It was rather a deceptive thing; one looked down and saw it coming up apparently very slowly—and then suddenly as it got closer it seemed to be coming uncomfortably fast. I do not pretend ever to have had any affection or lacked respect for "Archie", but he did not frighten me as much as the German fighters did. I was always frightened of fighters and, when possible, if my observer saw them in time, used to exercise that discretion which is the better part of valour by telling the battery I was ranging to hold hard a bit (M.Q. was the code for that, if I remember rightly) and coming back well our side of the Line where one was seldom followed. These interruptions did not often last long; there were usually too many of our fighters about for the enemy to want to hang around in our vicinity. Sometimes when we had a special job on hand that involved relatively deep penetration—orbiting for a longish time well over the other side—we used to have an unofficial arrangement with a neighbouring fighter squadron for close escort. This was frowned on from on high, but actually was the only way of getting the job done; without it one was at best always being chased off by enemy fighters, and at worst shot down.

I was never actually shot down I'm glad to say. There were occasions when I had to make hurried unorthodox landings away from home as a result of unfriendly attentions by the

3

Germans. One such was when I was shot through the petrol tank doing a low wire-reconnaissance north of Oppy Wood, and just managed to scrape in to a little airfield at Mont St. Eloi, soaked in petrol and with a "dead stick". But I was never properly shot down, which I suppose is just as well, since we had no parachutes in aeroplanes in 1917, so we could not get out and walk if we got into trouble.

★   ★   ★

The accidental collision with one of our own or the enemy's shells on its way to a ground target was a different sort of hazard and actually, I suspect, rather an expensive one. There were at least two aircraft in 5 Squadron during my time that were known to be destroyed in this way. One I saw happen and a very unpleasant sight it was—one minute an old R.E.8 flying quietly along within a few hundred yards of me, and next minute it just disintegrated in a terrific explosion—the shell no doubt had an instantaneous fuse. I was luckier; I was twice hit, once I know by one of our own shells and once I think by one of the enemy's, and got away with it on both occasions. The zone in which we had to fly was roughly from 3,000 to 5,000 feet above the ground—high enough to be out of effective small-arm range and not so high that one could not distinguish the detail of the targets; and that zone just about coincided with the upper reaches of the heavier natures of artillery. One got accustomed to seeing shells in clear weather, passing in both directions, and sometimes felt the bump caused by air displaced by a heavy shell passing close to the aircraft. We worked out a theory about the safest place to fly actually during a battle when there was a great deal of miscellaneous metal flying around; the idea was that there was a triangle of comparative safety—a triangle with curved sides if such a thing can be imagined; one side was represented by the shells of our own and another by those of the enemy barrage, crossing each other a few hundred feet from the ground; the upper side was the trajectory of the longer-range stuff, mostly counter-battery fire.

The trouble, of course, was that sooner or later one had to turn homewards through what the eye of imagination was liable to depict as a dense curtain of shells—and actually it was sometimes pretty thick. One of the occasions on which I met a shell was when doing just that during an offensive by the Canadian Corps in front of Lens in August 1917. I had been on counter-battery work for about two-and-a-half hours that rather thundery afternoon, while an intensive artillery duel raged and huge clouds of smoke and dust from burning Lens and the pock-marked desert to the west of the town drifted westwards on the warm wind. In due course I decided to call it a day as petrol was getting short, and turned West for home. Almost at once I was hit by what must have been one of our heavy howitzer shells, fortunately not with an instantaneous fuse, for it tore an enormous hole in my starboard upper wing and went on its way without exploding. It was an alarming moment; but the old R.E.8 was pretty robust as wood and canvas aircraft went. She wallowed a bit, dropped the injured wing but got me safely home, I flying—like Agag—very delicately and slowly, making as few turns as possible.

* * *

My nearest approach to being properly shot down was earlier that summer. My observer on that occasion was Freddy Tymms, a quiet, efficient and entirely imperturbable individual who was the oldest and best observer in No. 5 Squadron at the time. That fine June morning we had been detailed to fill in some gaps in the latest photographic mosaic of the counter-battery area and, perhaps rather unwisely, had gone over by ourselves without arranging for fighter escort or cover patrol. It was a fine summer morning with about five-tenths cloud at 4,500 feet and we were below it—inevitably as we had to get the photographs; and, as so often in such conditions, we were jumped on out of the clouds by five red Albatross, which I at first mistook for our own Nieuport fighters. Three of them were pretty chicken-hearted and sheered off at the first burst from Freddy's Lewis gun; the other two were better and stuck to us—one in particular got on our tail and I simply could not shake him off. He may have been Richtofen for all I know, or perhaps his Second-in-Command, Captain Hermann Goering, who was later to earn such an unenviable reputation as the (fortunately very bad) Commander-in-Chief of the Luftwaffe in Hitler's war. Anyway he was jolly good and frightened me very badly. I remember doing a rather frantic Immelmann turn to try to shake him off; but when I looked back, there he still was, the goggled face behind the windscreen and the two machine guns still spitting lead at us. He made a lot of holes in us but fortunately nowhere vital; in retrospect I can't think how it was that Freddy did not get him with one of the four double-drums of Lewis gun ammunition that he let off—perhaps it was my fault for throwing the aeroplane about too much. At last, when we were at about 500 feet and the small arms from the German trenches were joining in (and, incidentally, Freddy had just told me very calmly that he was out of ammunition!), my Squadron-Commander, Eric Tyson,[1] joined in from above; he was up on some other job and, seeing one of his squadron in trouble, sailed in and the enemy sheered off.

*   *   *

Well—it all sounds a bit dangerous, but it was not as lethal as all that; our casualties were not too heavy. The Corps Squadrons were not the glamour boys of 1914–18 in the air; that, as in the early stages of a later war, was reserved for the fighters— I think on the whole deservedly. It is true, of course, that the sole reason for their existence was to enable us to do our job. 1914–18 was an "Army Co-operation" war and the other activities of the Air Forces were mainly concerned to contribute to that end, though for those who had eyes to see they could be seen as a foretaste of what was to be real air warfare a generation later. Of one thing I am sure—the dangers that we had to

---

[1] A large, silent, very gallant chap—son of the then Bursar of Westminster School.

face were pretty small beer compared with those endured by
our successors in 1939–45—particularly those in Bomber Command. They had some advantages no doubt—parachutes, for
instance, and self-sealing fuel tanks. But, having been through
both wars in the Air Service, I for one am thankful that we old
boys did our turn as active operational pilots in the Kaiser's war
rather than in Hitler's.

The first thing about Porter that struck one was his youth—he was really incredibly young. As a matter of fact I suppose he had been born only a year or so later than most of us. I was only just 20, but had an Ops. tour in the Middle East behind me and a little thin gold wound-stripe on the sleeve of my maternity jacket, and thought myself the hell of an old soldier. And from the day Porter joined my Flight, fresh from home just after the Battle of Vimy Ridge, I always felt somehow paternal about him—or perhaps it would be more accurate to say I felt like a College Prefect towards a particularly defenceless and immature new boy. He was so eager and so inexperienced—so brave and so willing. Long before I felt he had had enough experience on quiet, cushy sorties to fit him for the real business, he was aching to get into battle. When, for instance, a formation was being detailed for Counter-battery photographs, Porter would say "Ooo—*do* let me come too", as though one were laying on a picnic in Canaders up the river to Godstow and he could not bear to be out of it.

In appearance he was rather cherubic, with unruly fair hair, a wide smile and frank blue eyes behind steel-rimmed spectacles—he was short-sighted and I can't think how he had been passed for Service as a pilot. His father was a very senior Don and he had been nicely brought up—an only child—in a quiet home in North Oxford. He was a gunner, but had quickly transferred to the R.F.C. and this was his first experience of active service.

And he was a very bad pilot. I think it was probably those eyes, but anyway he really was bad. I have often kicked myself since for not having had the moral courage to get him taken off flying. But I think it would have broken his heart. He broke several aeroplanes—it was always rather a nerve-racking experience to watch him coming in to land. I made him do a lot of practice flying without a passenger, took him up several times to try to show him how to land a R.E.8, and then gave him a few soft, safe jobs with an experienced observer. There was a moment when I hardened my heart (I think it was after one of those occasions when he had wiped off an undercarriage and I was in rather a bad temper) and told him I was going to have him sent home; Porter's jaw dropped, he stared at me in unbelieving horror and his eyes actually filled with tears. Well—I mean, what could one do when that sort of thing happened? Anyway what I did (and I have now no doubt that I was wrong) was weaken and give him another chance. It might have been different in a single-seater squadron, but we had the R.E.8 and I should have had more consideration for the poor devils who had to go up with him.

Oddly enough the chap who was eventually detailed as his regular gunner didn't seem to mind. His name was Morris and he was an interesting and rather queer character—the only chap in my Flight whom I never really got to know, though I liked and respected him. He was a tall, fine-looking man, lean and brown and clean-shaven, who had refused to take a Commission—he was the only N.C.O. gunner in the Squadron as far as I remember. He was a "cat who walked by himself", moody and withdrawn and subject to sudden tempers. In one such he suddenly became mutinous and violently abusive, for which he collected a dose of Field Punishment No. 1, which included several hours a day strapped to the wheel of a limber in the open—a stupid and grossly undignified form of punishment which, of course, would not be tolerated for one moment to-day. But Morris came out of it taciturn and unruffled, apparently bearing no malice, and went on quietly and efficiently with his job as air gunner. An odd fish but, I always felt, a very nice chap if only one could get at him, past his barrier of reserve. No doubt he had something queer or tragic in his background, but I never discovered what it was. So to me he remained till the end just a jolly good gunner, who was liable once in a way to fly off the handle.

Morris evidently liked Porter—I think he felt protective towards him as so many of us did. They were as different as chalk and cheese, in appearance and character but, as apparent opposites so often seem to do, they had some odd affinity. I remember one summer evening standing with the two of them outside the hangars watching one of my aircraft taxi in after an artillery patrol. When the pilot had turned her alongside the hangar and shut off the engine, he slumped in his seat and it was found that he had taken an explosive bullet from an enemy fighter in his right arm, just below the shoulder. Morris was silent, saturnine and practical as he helped to lift the pilot out; Porter was bubbling over with concern and sympathy—"Oh! poor fellow, my word how awful. Do you think he'll be all right?" and so on. Incidentally the pilot on that occasion was Lieut. A. P. M. Sanders; little did either of us think that warm summer evening in Artois that thirty-five years later I should be C.A.S. and he my Deputy, five years after another Great War against the same enemy. He had to have the arm amputated that night in a nearby Field Hospital; but anyone who knows Sir Arthur Sanders to-day will testify that he can do at least as much with one arm as most people with two—including tying a tiny dry fly on to a 3X cast.

Well—the summer dragged on with its long series of mostly quite useless minor actions on our Corps front from Fresnoy to Gavrelle—bitter, costly little battles to take or retake a few thousand square yards of shell-torn ground which could hardly have mattered less. In retrospect those actions seem to epitomize the utter beggary of the military art in 1917. Oppy Wood, a little stinking square of blackened match-sticks in a sea of mud, was attacked again and again to "widen the salient" created by our capture of Fresnoy. Then Fresnoy was recaptured by the Germans. Further South the Royal Naval Division hung desperately on to Gavrelle windmill against repeated German counter-attacks, and the chemical works at Rouex changed hands half a dozen times. All nearly completely useless waste of life. But by about the end of June things settled down into a semi-peace of exhaustion and the long sunny days went by with nothing much going on—desultory shelling of each others' trenches, counter-battery bombardment and the odd trench raid to get identifications and keep the enemy stirred up. A lot of that was pretty useless and only accentuated the discomforts of life in the trenches. The French Army, who fought like tiger-cats in a battle, believed in a policy of live and let live in between battles. In our Army there was a theory that such was bad for morale and sapped the fighting spirit of the troops. I suppose that as usual the truth lay somewhere between the two, though I think the French were more nearly right than we. Actually it depended to some extent on the Corps and Divisional Commanders and there were some sectors on our front where, between battles, there was a sort of unwritten understanding that if the enemy were not unnecessarily tiresome to us, we would equally refrain from being unduly offensive to him. I can't say I ever noticed that the morale of the troops was weakened by that—in fact I'd have thought rather the reverse; but then, I'm not an infantryman and don't know.

Our Corps Commander at that time was Lt.-General Sir Walter Congreve, V.C., who certainly did not lack the offensive spirit. He was a charming, courtly person, as polite to very young officers as to his equals in rank and age, but there were occasions on which I confess I did not relish his company. I commanded the Squadron for a couple of months that summer in the absence of Eric Tyson on sick leave; and General Congreve thought it would be good for the Commander of his Corps Squadron to accompany him sometimes on his visits to the front-line troops. I was all for seeing how the poor lived and used to enjoy going up to battery positions on off days, discussing our mutual problems and drinking whisky and water in the battery dug-out. But it would be idle to pretend that I enjoyed those tours in the trenches with old Congreve. He had a nose like a beagle for trouble. We'd be standing in a

3*

nice quiet trench nattering to a Company Commander, when the Boche would start putting over mortar fire somewhere along the line. "Come on," Congreve would say, "I think we should go and see what's happening." I could not have cared less what was happening as long as it didn't happen to me. But off we would trudge, I trailing miserably behind him thinking, "All very well for them as likes it, but what the hell has this got to do with a poor R.F.C. officer?" But Congreve was a great and gallant soldier whom it was a privilege to know and serve under.

Meanwhile little Porter was gaining experience and becoming a bit less dangerous—I'm afraid one can't put it higher than that; but the taciturn Morris seemed quite happy with him. One would see them walking in to report after a sortie (we did not call them sorties in those days, by the way), Porter talking away nineteen to the dozen and Morris putting in the odd word and even an occasional smile. Then one day during a quiet period they were sent off on a counter-battery patrol. Porter's own aircraft was undergoing overhaul and I lent him mine, which had a silly mascot—a fluffy toy dog, wired to a centre-section strut and wearing round his tummy a silk stocking belonging to a very pretty cousin of mine with whom at the time I imagined myself to be in love. I saw them off from the hangars—and they did not come back. Later in the day 13 Squadron, on our right, rang up to say one of their chaps on patrol had seen an R.E.8 shot down in flames by a couple of Hun fighters—they thought it was just inside the enemy line on Greenland Hill. And that evening we were told by Corps that the wreckage was in no-man's-land just south of Gavrelle, where the front line trenches were unusually far apart, and a stretcher party from a battalion of the Rifle Brigade had brought in the bodies.

Now, that aeroplane of mine was carrying a camera fitted with a special lens that we valued highly. It was a German lens that, I regret to say, produced better photographs than any of our Service issue cameras, and had been taken from an enemy reconnaissance aircraft shot down on the Vimy ridge some months before. It struck me that since it had been possible to bring in the bodies, one might perhaps be able to retrieve this valuable lens, and the Squadron Photographic Officer thought it might have survived even being shot down in flames—anyway it was well worth trying. In this warm weather of late summer that was sometimes a sort of somnolent doldrum in the middle of the day when the Germans (or so we imagined) were having their sauerkraut and sausage. So next morning I set off in an old Crossley tender, calling on the way at Corps H.Q. for guidance and advice, to see if I could retrieve the lens. I also wanted to bring back the bodies for burial at the little cemetery near the airfield. I was directed to the Headquarters of the Brigade holding that bit of the front, which was located in the support line, behind the Point du Jour. I was kindly received, though no one seemed to know where the bodies were; the Brigadier thought there should be no difficulty about reaching the wreckage—things were pretty quiet just now and it wasn't far beyond our forward trenches—and produced as a guide and escort the Brigade interpreter, an elderly and imperturbable bearded Frenchman in a blue uniform.

We left the tender in dead ground beside the Arras–Fresnes road and walked forward over the crest into full view of the front lines and enemy country beyond them. Well, I thought, I suppose this is all right, though I'm not accustomed to viewing "Hunland" at close quarters from this angle. But the sun shone, a lark was singing and a warm breeze ruffled the grass and cornflowers by the roadside; somewhere up Oppy way a machine-gun stammered and stopped; we heard from behind the occasional "Boom" of a ranging howitzer, the flutter of the shell overhead and the distant "Crrrump" as it burst on some enemy battery position two or three thousand yards in front of us. Otherwise all very peaceful and summery. My French friend trudged stolidly on, smoking a pipe. "Don't vorry," he said placidly, "they don't vorry us—long as ve don't move around more than two or three men together." But I confess to some relief when we dropped into a communication trench and soon found ourselves in the Battalion H.Q. dug-out where, having been warned of our coming by Brigade, they had a guide waiting to take us to the point in the front line nearest to the wreckage.

I peered rather unhappily over the parapet under the rim of my tin helmet. To hell with this, I thought, this isn't my line of country at all—why was I such a bloody fool as to be so keen about this blasted lens? But there I was, there was no turning back now; the elderly Frenchman was still quite unperturbed, his pipe still between his teeth. Actually I think the ground between us and the wreck must have been dead to direct fire from the German line; and clambering over the parapet I crawled in the Frenchman's wake through high, rank grass and poppies to the still smouldering pile that yesterday morning had been my nice aeroplane. Now to find the camera—or what was left of it; we each had a walking stick and, crawling on hands and knees, were poking about in the mess when suddenly I saw, glaring balefully at me from the ashes, a large brown eye! I felt a prickle on the back of my neck and something turned slowly over in my tummy; and then I remembered—the mascot, the poor little windswept, rather grubby toy dog! but it was a nasty moment.

We were in luck. We did find the camera, not completely destroyed, and bore it back in triumph to the waiting tender— and that lens in another camera continued to give yeoman service, as far as I know for the duration of the war. We called at Brigade on the way back to drop the interpreter, thank the Brigadier for his help and make further inquiries about the bodies. "Oh yes," said the Staff Captain, "those two poor chaps who were shot down yesterday—I hear one of your chaps with a V.C. was asking about them this morning—oh, I see it was you—come on, I'll show you where they are." I need hardly say I had not got a V.C.; being endowed with a generous allowance of the instinct for self-preservation I never looked or felt remotely like earning the V.C. But some months before I had been fortunate in the lucky dip for a Belgian honour, the Order of Leopold, of which the ribbon was much the same colour as the V.C. Incidentally the parade at which my decoration, amongst others, was presented happened when I was on leave; my observer, Freddy Tymms, had at the same time been awarded the Belgian Order of the Crown, so he was kissed on both cheeks by a rather bristly Belgian General not once but twice—once for his own decoration and once for mine which he accepted as my proxy.

The Staff Captain I suppose should have known that the V.C. ribbon is worn in front of the Military Cross and not after it— I think this was before the days when the miniature cross is worn on the ribbon to distinguish the V.C. from other ribbons of similar colour. But who was I to disillusion him? So I basked in bogus glory; and having lifted what was left of poor Porter and Morris reverently into the back of the tender, drove sadly home through the gathering dusk to our little airfield at Acq.

6   Trenchard and the Birth of the Royal Air Force, 1918

The headline of a derogatory article on Trenchard in (I need hardly say) a Beaverbrook newspaper asks: "Was this man a hero or a prima donna?" The answer, of course, is that he was both. The prima donna—passionately involved, unpredictable, temperamental, often difficult to deal with, sometimes inclined to be egocentric, but supremely good at his job; the hero—a man whose physical and moral courage were unsurpassed; and in both, one of the few really great men of our time.

As one of his young officers (everyone was a "young officer" to "Boom" until we were about 50), and one who, when eventually I found myself holding the appointment in which more than twenty years before I had served him closely as a Staff Officer, never found his advice anything but welcome and helpful, I have written of him elsewhere: "It is difficult to define that quality of real greatness. Self-confidence without a trace of arrogance; a contemptuous yet not intolerant disregard for anything mean or petty; the capacity to shuffle aside the non-essentials and put an unerring finger on the real core of a problem or the true quality of a man, a sort of instinct for the really important point; a selfless devotion to the cause of what he believed to be true and right. Trenchard has all those characteristics and, above all, a shining sincerity. Many people have disagreed with him. Some of them have lived to admit with the passage of time that he was right and they wrong. None of them will suggest that he is ever anything but entirely disinterested and sincere."

In that last sentence I was wrong. Someone has made that

suggestion; but I am probably not alone in regarding abuse from that quarter as a compliment.

He had his faults, of course. Who has not? He was sometimes unduly secretive—a cat that walked by himself—and his method of approach to a problem was sometimes a little tortuous and difficult to understand. Sometimes he observed to a fault Lord Fisher's maxim: "Never explain".

In some ways he resembled his great contemporary, Churchill; few of us who knew both men were very surprised at the outcome of that meeting in 1940 that Mr. Boyle describes.[1] He was sometimes carried away by his enthusiasms, as when in 1929 he could not resist circulating as a Cabinet paper the famous "last will and testament", which created unnecessary difficulties for Salmond and did no good to the cause he had at heart. He would surely have agreed that the fact of his judgment of men and affairs being so seldom wrong was due in part to the quiet wisdom of Lady Trenchard. He had very strong and usually sound views of his own which, in his later days when no longer in a position of responsibility, he was inclined to press without sufficient regard for the squalid realities of life. His insistence that we should be bombing Germany in the early months of the war was no doubt partly due to the fact that Ellington and Newall had not kept either him or Salmond well enough informed; but he was hard to convince, and I, as Director of Plans, sometimes found myself at that time arguing hotly with him that, however admirable his strategic idea, to try to put it into effect when our resources were still totally inadequate, could only result in ignominious and costly failure.

This was not the only occasion when his bold spirit got the better of his judgment—I remember him being cross with me for refusing to agree that it would be a good idea to send an armoured division down the autobahn during the Berlin blockade.

He was almost incapable of the slightest genuflexion in the

[1] *Trenchard,* by Andrew Boyle, Collins, 1962.

house of Rimmon. I don't think political sense was his strongest point, though he was often shrewd in his relations with politicians, and was always aware of the importance of getting them on his side in his struggles to preserve the infant Air Force after World War I. He had his own way of side-stepping political opposition. I remember well the occasion when he wanted to increase our air strength in Egypt by sending No. 6 Squadron to the Canal Zone, and consulted the Permanent Under-Secretary at the Foreign Office as to whether there would be any political objections. Sir William Tyrell said that we could not possibly approach the Egyptian Government in that sense at that particular moment. "I then explained to Sir William Tyrell," ran Boom's subsequent minute on the file, "that in point of fact I had already moved No. 6 Squadron to Egypt *in a small way and on a very low basis.*" What he meant, of course, was that he had done it on his own responsibility without any fuss or publicity, and no dog in Egypt had barked, and that being so, Tyrell was quite happy to accept the position. Those words in italics became for Boom's "young officers" a sort of code-word for this sort of tactic which often saves so much bother and avoids putting Ministers in the position of having to make (or refuse to make) desirable but uncomfortable decisions.

Whatever Trenchard's faults may have been, I class him with Churchill and Smuts as one of the three greatest men I have been privileged to know.

The point I want to deal with in this note is Trenchard's attitude to the formation of an autonomous Air Force in April, 1918. That point is also misunderstood—though not so grossly misrepresented—in another more responsible and sympathetic review in another newspaper. There, too, the reviewer quotes Beaverbrook's accusation that Trenchard "was the father who tried to strangle the infant at birth though he got credit for the grown man", and his headline reads: "Reluctant apostle of air power." On the contrary, it was not air power of which he was a reluctant apostle, but a political expedient in organization

which he was afraid might fatally handicap air power in playing its part in what was the vital issue in the spring of 1918—
namely, winning the war. Certainly he was an Army man; of
course he attached supreme importance at that time to support
of the Army. Why not, for God's sake? By the spring of 1918
what else could win the war? What else but the gigantic
struggle on land might even still result in our losing it?

A key to his thinking can be found in an article by him in the
Army Quarterly in 1921. "All bombing," he wrote then, "even
when carried out on very different and apparently independent
objectives, must be co-ordinated with the efforts that are being
made by the land or sea forces, both as to the selection of objectives and as to the time at which the attacks shall take place . . .
It is utterly wrong and wasteful to look upon them as entirely
separate duties." It was his conviction that air power could best
contribute to victory on land and at sea, as well as having a
direct impact on an enemy will to resist, if it were not split up
between the two older Services (which he well knew would
mean that the Air Service would suffer the fate of the Tank
Corps between the wars), that inspired his struggles to retain an
autonomous Air Force after the Armistice.

It is true that if the merger between the R.F.C. and the
R.N.A.S. had not come when it did, it might never have come,
or have come too late, and we might well have been defeated
in that other war that was to come twenty years later. But was
anyone to know that in 1917–18? As Mr. Boyle rightly points
out, Smuts and Cowdray, Weir and David Henderson were
men of vision who were right for the wrong reasons; Trenchard, as he himself with characteristic honesty has admitted,
was wrong, but for the right reasons. I can only say that I hope
that I, in his place, would have been equally wrong for the
same reasons. What determined Trenchard in his opposition at
the time was none of the baser motives that little men have
imputed to him, but four factors; his sound sense of strategic
priorities—the idea codified in the manuals as the principle of
concentration on whatever is vital at the time; his intimate

knowledge of the situation in France and the weakness of the French Army; his utter loyalty to Haig; and his no less profound mistrust of so many of the politicians in London. All these Mr. Boyle brings out clearly and competently in his book.

This seems to me the really crucial point to understand about Trenchard in those days, not merely to refute malicious gossip, not just as a matter of history, but because it contains so many lessons which we should do well to remember to-day. In what follows I draw on a chapter on strategic concentration in a book called *Air Power and Armies*,[2] which I wrote nearly thirty years ago; and it may be worth recording that I received in India a warm letter of approval of that book from Trenchard, referring in particular to that chapter.

The political pressure for air bombardment of German cities stemmed largely from the urge for reprisals after the Gotha raids on London in June, 1917. Nevertheless, Weir and Cowdray had been pressing before that for a policy of long-range bombing against Germany. It is not to depreciate their foresight to point out that their ideas were based on the fallacy that there would soon be a great surplus of aircraft over and above the needs of the other two Services. As Mr. Boyle reminds us, even the Smuts Report, which was the decisive factor in the eventual formation of the Royal Air Force, was based on that fallacy. Trenchard even then had few illusions about the results in that context of the efforts of the Air Board which, since early 1916, was supposed to have been co-ordinating and bringing some order out of the chaos of the separate War Office and Admiralty activities in the field of air supply. For many months he had been trying to make bricks without straw, to match with the morale and courage of his pilots the results of superior German production, and to maintain on a shoestring the tenuous hold on air superiority gained during the Somme battle. The tenuous nature of that hold is a vivid memory to those of us who flew in France in the spring of 1917. He had constantly seen all estimates and promises falsified in the event.

[2] Oxford University Press, 1934.

Salmond, on taking over from Henderson on the Army Council in October, 1917, put a quick finger on the truth. The supplies and contracts branch of the Air Board, he soon realized, were people who lived permanently in clouds of bright theoretical figures. "Practically not a single one of their estimates has been met," he told Trenchard, to whom this certainly was not news, "their programmes . . . have not had the slightest chance of being fulfilled." In this connection Northcliffe's report that "it is unlikely that more than 5,000 fighting planes fitted with Liberty engines will be in France before July, 1918" (about ten times the total that were in front-line service at the Armistice five months later), has a familiar ring to those of us who remember Beaverbrook's equally fantastic assurances about the supply of aircraft from America twenty-two years after.

Nevertheless, this idea of the surplus persisted, and in his book[3] Sykes tells us that "fortunately in 1918, when I was C.A.S., we managed to secure a margin and formed the Independent Air Force in June of that year". On this I wrote in 1933, "Sir Frederick Sykes . . . has [not] offered any solution of the problem of how, when, or by whom it is to be decided that 'the necessary uses of aircraft' by the other Services have been adequately ensured and that a surplus is now available for other uses . . . both cases are in fact fundamentally and dangerously unsound." Duval of the French General Staff had said the same thing in different words to a sub-committee of the Supreme War Council in 1918. "I shall be grateful," he said, "to any authority capable of determining the limit of what is necessary to the winning of a battle. Great commanders have always solved this problem by making use of every resource within reach."

I am sure that I—and even more Trenchard—will be acquitted of the fallacious belief that the land or sea theatres of war are necessarily always the vital point. But the fact is that even in those early days Trenchard understood more clearly than anyone else the importance of what is the supremely important

[3] *Aviation in Peace and War.*

principle of air warfare—concentration of the maximum effort on whatever may be the really vital point at the time; and in early 1918 that was unmistakably the battle in France. We who have lived through the past twenty years must surely know well enough that there was not then the remotest chance of achieving any decisive effect by bombing the fringe areas of Germany with the few stick-and-string biplanes and rudimentary bombs of that day. The one and only place where, by the spring of 1918, the war could be won—and where there were anxious moments when it still looked as though it might be lost—was the Western Front in France.

What was the situation there when this great surplus was theoretically accumulating, when Sykes was "securing his margin", and when politicians in London were pressing on with the formation of a new independent Service free from the trammels of Army control? On 21st March the Germans launched their great offensive towards Amiens and the Channel ports; early in April Haig was drafting his famous "Backs to the wall" order.[4] "No sooner had one terrific German offensive been brought to a standstill than another was launched elsewhere; and the allied armies were literally gasping for breath. Invalids, 'C.3 men', airmen of balloon sections, cooks and batmen were taking their places in the line; and the allied resources in personnel and material were strained almost to breaking point."[5] G.H.Q. in France were pleading for bombers to help stem the enemy's advance by disrupting his communications, but Sykes and his Air Staff said they had not enough aircraft! Where was the famous margin?

Who can be surprised that Trenchard, deeply imbued as he was with the desperate character of the struggle in France and utterly loyal to his old chief Haig, wholly and understandably unimpressed by the earlier efforts of the Air Board and know-

---

[4] The last time I saw the original manuscript of this famous order was in Philip Sassoon's lovely house in Park Lane, since demolished. I wonder what has happened to it?

[5] *Air Power and Armies*, p. 76.

ing the truth about this mythical "surplus", and fresh from that disgraceful interview with Rothermere and Northcliffe, could feel little enthusiasm for a reorganization which he thought might only make matters worse, and anyway did not believe could be permanent. If he had thought only of his own advancement, he must have recognized it as a great opportunity for him personally.

Historians will long debate whether Haig's persistence in the desperately costly summer and autumn battles of 1917 was decisively influenced by Pétain's secret disclosure to him of the mutinous condition of the French Army after the Nivelle fiasco. What is, to my personal knowledge, in no doubt whatever is that Trenchard, as a result of his own experience behind the French front in July and of his intimate relationship with Haig, was utterly convinced that this was so. That only added fuel to the flames of his determination not to let the Army down.

In that belief, and in his loyalty to Haig, he never wavered till the end of his life. I remember well an occasion when in 1942 Walter Lippmann came to London and I thought it would interest him and Trenchard to meet each other. We dined at my house in London and before dinner, over the wartime ration of sherry, the old man was in splendid form. Somehow the conversation turned to Haig. Trenchard suddenly said how he wished that Haig had lived to see the fall of France in 1940. And when Walter, not unnaturally, asked him to elaborate upon that somewhat curious theme, Boom snapped, looking very fierce: "The justification of Passchendaele." And then his rugged old face dissolved into that charming smile. "D'you see?" he added, in a ruminative rumble.

If we add to all this his failure to understand Curzon, his mistrust of Lloyd George and of politicians as a tribe, and the effect upon a soldier of his upright character and utter integrity of that appalling interview with the Press Barons, then we, who in our day were lucky enough to serve under a very different type of political master, can only marvel, not at his lack of enthusiasm about the new organization but at the sense of duty which led him, against all his personal inclinations, to agree to serve under a man like Rothermere.

It is unhappily typical of a certain class of popular newspaper today to "debunk" the great, to make out that Trenchard, having "used every possible argument to prevent the bombing of Germany", subsequently went back on his earlier convictions when "in 1918 he himself was put in charge of the bombing". It is perhaps unnecessary to defend Boom against that calumny, but thrown mud tends to stick. Mr. Boyle makes it quite clear how, after his resignation as C.A.S. under Rothermere, he at first refused the command of the Independent Air Force (what we should now call the Strategic Air Force engaged in the bombing of Germany) on the characteristic grounds that there was already a good man—Newall,[6] Trenchard's appointee— in command at Ochey and that he should remain under the G.O.C. in France (i.e. indirectly under Haig) instead of under the newly created Air Staff in London. When under pressure he accepted the command a week or so later, he was largely influenced by the feeling that he, more than anyone else, could use the force to help Foch and Haig win their decisive battles. He made it quite clear in his letter of acceptance that he did not agree with the policy of an independent bombing force at that time, but, having stated his objections, could not any longer reconcile it with his conscience as a soldier to do anything but his best to make a success of a policy that had been decided over his head.

So far from "using every possible argument to prevent the bombing of Germany", he had always favoured that course when the time was ripe and the resources were available. It was two years earlier that he had asked for ten squadrons of long-range bombers, and a year after that not one had materialized. It was he who had acquired and laid out the complex of airfields in the Nancy area when he was G.O.C. in France. It was under his direction that Newall and his 41st Wing had been bombing

[6] Later Marshal of the Royal Air Force Lord Newall, C.A.S., 1937 to 1940.

Germany since October. In November, 1917, he had written: "I want to bomb Germany, but please remember that if we lose half our machines doing so, the good morale effect which is three-quarters of the work, will be on the German side and not ours." (This is genuine vintage Trenchard English). "I am in no way trying to upset the policy of the War Cabinet for bombing Germany with a large number of machines. What I am trying to do is to do it efficiently and the crux of the whole matter seems to me to be whether we are going to have efficient machines to do it with." (I still wonder whether he meant efficient or sufficient.)

Mr. Boyle sums it up well. Trenchard's concern was "to convince the War Cabinet by deeds that the R.F.C.'s greatest need was a steady flow of supplies to increase the Ochey Wing's effectiveness, not an Act of Parliament to declare its independence". That he did not share Smuts's optimistic view, based on a wholly misleading estimate by the Air Board of the possibilities of production, that air power could be a war-winning factor on its own *in the circumstances of that time* surely testifies only to the sound objectivity of his judgment.

However all this may be, the memory of Trenchard—prima donna and hero, soldier and strategist, and father of the Royal Air Force—will rest secure in the respect and affection of all who were privileged to know and serve with him.

There was something about the old North-West Frontier of
India that had a romantic appeal I think to all reasonably adventurous young men in the early nineteen twenties—I know there
was for me. I had been brought up on *Kim* and *The Drums of
the Fore and Aft*, and stories of the Afridi campaign of 1897 in
the Tirah; and characters like Mahbub Ali and Piper Findlater
(whom my father had seen winning his V.C. at Dargai) were
my special heroes as a small boy. So early in 1921, after a year
as a flying instructor at Netheravon, I was more than happy to
find myself on board H.M. Transport *Circassia* out of Tilbury,
an antique troopship eastward-bound for India and the Straits.

All trooping nowadays is done by air—which, of course,
saves a lot of time as well as being less expensive and more
comfortable, anyway for "other ranks" and their families. But
I can't help feeling we lost something when the last sea troopers
were laid up. For the officers it was a pleasant interlude; nothing
in the way of responsibility but the odd day as ship's orderly
officer—except for the less fortunate few in charge of drafts;
the food was very good and the cabins quite comfortable; one
made new friends in the bar and at the card-tables, and there
were enough mild gaieties to keep us amused—too many if one
was not careful to avoid the enthusiasts who were always getting up games of deck-tennis or quoits. For the men it was
rather different, but on the whole I think they enjoyed it; three
or four weeks with few fatigues or duties, interminable games
of "Housy-Housy"[1] on deck, and the occasional ship's concert.
But I have sometimes wondered what modern troops and their
families would have to say about the accommodation endured

---

[1] No-one then dreamt that 45 years later people in this country would be
spending millions a year on the brainless occupation now known as Bingo.

by their predecessors forty-five years ago in peace-time—
one can put up with anything in war. A couple of years later I
came home in another museum-piece—the old *Assaye*—in
the officers' sick-bay, which was a little space partitioned off
in a troop-deck on the water-line, and I must say it was pretty
squalid.

However, standards were lower in those days and nobody
really minded. They groused a bit—the comments from the
soldiers' wives when, as orderly officer, one went round the
troop-decks at mealtimes and asked the usual "Any com-
plaints?" were pungent, but always good-humoured; nobody
was any the worse for it. And in due course *Circassia* docked at
Bombay in the land of my birth; and half a dozen of us young
Air Force officers boarded the Frontier Mail for Lahore and
points North.

*   *   *

The little cantonment of Parachinar lies at the head of the
Kurram valley, about 6,000 feet above sea-level a few miles
from the Peiwar Kotal, a pass on one of the old trade routes
between Afghanistan and India through which Lord Roberts
marched his army in the Afghan war of 1878. It was a pleasant
place lying in a great amphitheatre of rugged hills, flanked on
the north side by the snow-capped massif of the Safed Koh and
reached by a road from Kohat and Thal which followed the
river bed, winding now through arid gorges, now through
small terraced fields green with young crops, and under the
shade of willow, walnut and *chenar*. The locals were amiable
and relatively peaceful people—Shi'a Mussulmans surrounded
on all sides by unfriendly and more warlike Sunni tribes, and
with some admixture of English and Irish blood, a legacy from
Roberts's Army. It was not normally a regular military station;
but when I joined 20 Squadron there in April '21, rattling up
from Kohat on the little, dusty, narrow-gauge railway to Thal
and thence on by road, the Frontier had not yet settled down
after the bitterly contested Waziristan operations of 1919–20.
So there was still at Parachinar a perimeter camp holding a

Brigade of the Indian Army—two Indian and one British battalions—and my new Squadron of the R.A.F. with a bare, stony and, by modern standards, ludicrously small airfield.

As a centre of population the town of Parachinar had no claim to distinction. There was the usual rather scruffy little agglomeration of mud houses, the odd mosque, the graveyard outside the walls with its crumbling whitewashed shrine and little tattered flags flapping on long bamboo poles. There was the Serai where the camel caravans from Afghanistan rested after coming down through the Peiwar; they used to pay off their tribal guards in kind, in the form of Bokhara or Merv rugs which one could then buy very cheap in the bazaar—I have one or two still. And a bit up the hill outside the town was the Headquarters, barracks and Officers' Mess of the Kurram Militia, the local Irregular Corps whose job it was to enforce law and order in the Valley and garrison the little "Beau Geste" forts that guarded the road and the Afghan frontier.

*　　*　　*

The Frontier Irregular Militias were a great feature of the North-West Frontier in the old days, and still are. Some years after Partition I dropped in to call on one of them, old friends of mine, and found them still going strong under Pakistani officers of much the same wiry, adventurous type that I had known in the old days when secondment to a Frontier Militia was much sought after by right-minded young British officers of the Indian Army. There were a number of these Corps scattered up and down the Frontier: the Zhob Militia with headquarters at Fort Sandeman in Baluchistan, the Wana Militia and the Tochi Scouts in Waziristan, the Kurram Militia, the Khyber Rifles and the Chitral Scouts. Officered by British regular officers, the non-commissioned officers and men were all Pathans, incredibly tough and hence well up to the fighting weight of the wild tribesmen among whom they lived. Every man a marksman, they moved like mountain goats and on a *ghasht*, or patrol, thought nothing of 30 or 40 miles a day across the jagged hills

and burning valleys of the Frontier. Not for them motor transport or any of the impedimenta nowadays considered indispensable for regular troops. They would move out at a moment's
notice with rifle and bandoliers, a water bottle, a *chupatti* or two
and a handful of raisins—and their British officers soon became
as tough as their men. They lacked the spit and polish of the
Brigade of Guards but they always looked neat and workman-
like, and their weapons were perfectly kept. They were cheerful
and immensely likeable rogues and their discipline—though
perhaps unorthodox by the standards of Caterham—was excellent; they could not afford to have it otherwise.

We of the R.A.F. always got on very well with the Frontier
Militias. We held unconventional views about control of the
Frontier, and the British officers of Militias for the most part
shared them. We thought that if They—the Powers in Delhi
and Simla—left Frontier control to us and the Militias, and kept
the Regular troops out of the tribal areas, then between us we
could well deal with the tribes who would thus be deprived of
the inducements to disorder represented by the presence of
troops.[2] The Pathan enjoyed these little wars that the Indian
Army were always laying on for him—on the average about
once a year; they were his national pastime—like soccer in
England—and the source of valuable loot, particularly Service
rifles which were so much better and more durable than the
faithful imitations (complete down to the number on the butt
plate) which were produced in the tribal factory on the Kohat
pass, where one could watch an old Pathan turning out a rifle-
barrel on a primitive lathe operated by a string tied to his big toe.

The Militias were quite a different kettle of fish, Pathans
themselves and up to all the tricks of the trade. While the Air
Force—the *Hawai Jehaz Wallahs*, the air ship fellows—was no
fun at all; no juicy columns to ambush, no perimeter camps to
snipe, no rifles to steal; fighting against us, as Air Marshal
Ludlow-Hewitt used to say, must have been as poor fun for the

[2] Actually this is how the Frontier is now controlled by the Pakistani
authorities; there are today no regular troops in the tribal areas.

Pathan as it would be for the toreador if the bull failed to put in an appearance in the ring. One must admit that these little Frontier wars were also very good for the bull—the Regular soldier. They were excellent training for all ranks. Except for the odd major campaign, like the Tirah in 1897 or Waziristan in 1920, they were not very expensive in casualties. And any Army that had regular opportunities for this sort of training, with ball ammunition instead of blank, could count itself lucky. So it was not unnatural that Army Headquarters failed to see altogether eye to eye with the R.A.F. on the subject of Frontier warfare, though I am bound to say there were other less sensible reasons for the violent opposition in the early days to the system of Air Control.[3]

★   ★   ★

The Kurram Militia officers' compound was an oasis of green shade on those bare, stony slopes between the foothills and the river. There were great trees, green lawns and flowers in profusion. The Mess itself was typical of its kind, comfortably furnished, with some of the atmosphere of an old London club —deep, well-worn leather chairs, dark crimson rugs from Central Asia, shining silver and polished tables, a faint smell of cigar smoke and the walls covered with pictures and prints, glass-fronted cases of old medals, and sporting trophies. It had an indigenous population of black cocker spaniels—some old Militia officer of days gone by had established a tradition of breeding them at Parachinar. Just uphill behind the Mess was the Political Agent's residence, which was notable for being not the usual bungalow but a two-storeyed, rather Edwardian-looking villa—an oddity on the Frontier. It had not, however, bowed to modernity to the extent of having what everyone now regards as perfectly ordinary plumbing. Indeed that was almost unknown in India in the early nineteen-twenties except, perhaps, in the houses of the Very Great—which I did not frequent as a very insignificant Flight Lieutenant—and of the wealthy in big cities like Bombay and Calcutta.

[3] See *The Central Blue*, pages 51 to 75.

As a matter of fact I always rather liked the arrangements for ablution in India—which survived till after I came home in 1937. One's bath was an oval tin tub with a couple of handles in a small room with a stone or concrete floor, the *gussel-khana*. The household staff included a *bhisti* ("You're a better man than I am Gunga Din") who heated the bath-water over an open fire in the compound or a mud stove in an out-building. The Bearer was the senior servant in the household and the Sahib's valet; and on coming home from the Club after tennis or polo one might hear him in the back regions saying in a low and rather urgent voice into the darkness, "Ooh Bhisti—Gussel— jeldi karo" (Bhisti—bath—bring it quickly) before he came in to unbuckle spurs and pull off boots. Then, having added cold water to taste, one would squat in the little tin tub, lathering and sponging and splashing water all over the floor and—any- way in the hot weather—finish up by tipping a bowl of cold water over one's shoulders.

After all, the long bath with its taps and plugs and gleaming gadgets which we now regard as an indispensable adjunct to civilized life is really something quite modern. I look back rather nostalgically upon the old hip-bath of my early youth— not so very early as all that now I come to think of it. I remem- ber particularly a house in Northamptonshire where I used to stay for hunt balls after World War I. One would come in from hunting and, after an enormous tea of crumpets and poached eggs and a drop of whisky in one's tea, would go up to change. No bathroom—as far as I remember there was not such a thing in the house; but even as a young bachelor guest I had a large bedroom, panelled in dark oak with a big four-poster bed with old rose damask hangings, rather part-worn but all the cosier. There was my tail coat and boiled shirt all nicely laid out, and a blazing fire; and in front of the fire a blanket on the floor and on the blanket the hip-bath, two large copper cans, one of hot and one of cold water, and a soap-dish. There was something cosily luxurious about bathing in front of a fire in one's own bed- room. The hip-bath called for a technique of its own but was much more comfortable and practical than it looked. Very pleasant—anyway for the bather; not so much fun for the maids who had to haul great cans of water upstairs and empty the bath afterwards; how selfish we were in those days! But it was all taken for granted—I suppose there were a dozen or more servants in that not very big house.

*　　*　　*

It is a far cry from Northamptonshire to the North-West Frontier, but in 1935 a page of history was turned; the first long bath made its appearance in the wild tribal area of Waziristan— a real long bath with taps! Its inauguration was the occasion of a beguiling episode which I always regret not having witnessed.

General Sir Kenneth Wigram, after a lifetime in the Service of India, was about to relinquish the command of Northern Army and go home on retirement. He was a great Indian Army officer, a dedicated soldier and a rather reserved austere character—a brother of that Lord Wigram (also originally of the Indian Army) who was private Secretary to King George V. One of his last official duties was to pay a farewell visit to the garrison of the great fortified cantonment of Razmak, in the heart of Waziristan; and, of course, he was accommodated in the guest-room of the Headquarters Mess—what I suppose we should now describe by that horrible term, the "V.I.P." quarter. And it was here that the hitherto unheard of luxury of a long bath had just been installed; indeed from what followed it seems clear that there had been something in the nature of a last-minute flap about getting it finished in time for the Army Commander's visit. Anyway, there it was in the V.I.P. *gussel-khana*, taps gleaming and the tub shining under a lovely new coat of glossy white enamel. The Razmak Brigade were understandably proud; in half a dozen Officers' Messes lean, hard-bitten Frontier warriors spoke in hushed whispers—Have you heard? a real bath—they'll be having a pull-and-release before we know where we are!

The General duly arrived with his escort of Armoured cars, and that evening a Guest night was laid on in the Headquarters Mess to which all the Senior officers of the garrison were invited to do honour to their retiring Commander. Dinner, as usual, was at 8 p.m. and by about a quarter to eight the company was assembled, having a glass of sherry and probably most of them inwardly cursing the old convention which forbade smoking in the ante-room before dinner. Five minutes to eight o'clock— five past—still no sign of the Army Commander. Eventually the Brigadier said to his Staff Captain, "Bill, you'd better go and see if there's anything he wants—he may have lost a collar stud—or perhaps his watch has stopped."

Outside the door of the guest-room the General's bearer, who was squatting on his hunkers, rose and salaamed—looking rather anxious. The Staff Captain knocked; no answer, so he went in. There was the General's mess-kit—scarlet jacket with the row of miniature medals hung over the chairback, overalls standing at the ready pulled down over the spurred Wellington boots, boiled shirt on the bed—but no General. The *gussel-khana* opened out of the bedroom; and there was the Army Commander, having pulled the plug to release the water, sitting in *puris naturalibus* in an empty bath. "I'm very glad to see you," said he, with a patience and good humour which might pardonably have deserted lesser men, "I'm afraid something rather odd has happened; the fact is I've stuck to this bath."

CRISIS! What had happened was that the General's bearer, unversed in these matters—and anyway how could he have known—had turned on the hot water first; and this, coming in contact with the very new coat of enamel had melted it into a sort of glue which, when the General sat down, had a most effectively adhesive effect on the skin of his behind.

The Brigadier, John Marshall, was a man whom years of Frontier warfare had accustomed to appreciating critical situations quickly and arriving at instantaneous decisions on occasions of grave emergency. On hearing the report from his Staff Officer, he remembered at once that fortunately the Officers'

Mess of the Indian Medical Service was close by, across the road from Brigade Headquarters. And, preserving (probably not without some difficulty) the disciplined gravity appropriate to the occasion, he said "Pop across and get a doctor—quick!" The Medical Officers were at dinner in the dining room. But in the ante-room was a chap in grey flannel bags and a tweed coat sitting in an arm-chair reading a newspaper. He was grabbed, hustled across the road, ushered protesting into the General's bathroom and told to do his stuff. "But damn it," he said, his face scarlet with indignation and embarrassment, "I've been trying to tell you—I'm not a doctor, I'm in the Ordnance Corps." CRISIS again! This time a real Medical Officer was torn away from his dinner, and in due course the poor General was prised off the bottom of the bath, patched up and left to get into his Mess kit.

*   *   *

But that was all much later on; Razmak was unheard of in the days when 20 Squadron was quartered at Parachinar. In those days the R.A.F. in India was going through a rather difficult time. The Government of India was characterized by a certain conservatism, in some respects no doubt beneficial but not in relation to this new Service, of which their experience was very limited. Retrenchment in Defence expenditure (as always following a war) was the order of the day. The R.A.F. in India was then administered by the Army Department and its vote was merely one not very important head in the Military Services' budget (there were, after all, a lot of more important things, liked horsed cavalry regiments, to be paid for); so it was perhaps natural that we should be a first victim of the axe. But however natural, it was carried to a ludicrous and inexcusable extreme when an accounting blunder in Simla was covered up by putting a complete embargo on all Air Force stores and spare parts from England. Considering that many of our aircraft were veterans of the War in France and had been shipped to India direct from Marseilles after the armistice, and that the third Afghan war and the campaign in Waziristan in 1920 had made pretty heavy demands on the squadrons, it is hardly surprising that the result within a few months was a situation of which Sir John Salmond had to report in 1922 that "the R.A.F. in India is to all extents and purposes non-existent as a fighting force".

It had not quite reached that point in the summer of 1921, but not very far off it. We were lucky in 20 Squadron if we had four of our ancient Bristol Fighters fit to take the air out of an establishment of twelve; and that was only done by the process known as cannibalizing—taking a propeller from one aircraft, a magneto from another and a wheel from a third to make the fourth capable of flying. One "economy" that we particularly resented was to make us rub along with one magneto fitted instead of the standard two—not very comfortable when operating over country in which an engine failure spelt inevitable crash. Army officers should not have been surprised when, after this early experience, some of us in the R.A.F. were later a bit touchy about any suggestion that an Air Force Command should ever again come under the control of the Army.

The effect on our training was obvious and inevitable—for example, the Squadrons in India were able to fly only about one-third of the hours per month averaged by those in Iraq. Its effect on discipline was, perhaps equally inevitably, somewhat adverse; to keep about twenty high-spirited and keen young flying officers in a remote Frontier valley with very little flying, and equally little other useful work to make up for it, not unnaturally tended to induce a somewhat piratical atmosphere. We span for mahseer in the Kurram river, shot chikor in the foothills of the Safed Koh, played cricket on a coir matting pitch stretched on the airfield, and polo on a very rough and sloping ground half a mile or so outside the perimeter. I bought my first and very cheap polo ponies, a showy little bay Arab stallion and an aged flea-bitten grey with a mouth like reinforced concrete by the name of Fazl Din. The grey's previous owner was the Colonel of the 2nd Cameronians—also then quartered at Parachinar. It was related that on the Proclamation parade

4

the year before, the feu-de-joie[4] that terminated the proceedings had so affronted Fazl Din (he was then officiating as the Commanding Officer's charger) that he had departed—complete with Colonel—at high speed and did not pull up till about four miles from the parade ground. Judging by several of his later performances on—or rather off—the polo ground at Parachinar and subsequently at Umballa, I can quite believe it.

These distractions, however, were inadequate compensation for a severe shortage of work, which is always bad for discipline. We were not, I think, naturally undisciplined; we were a mixed lot, but those twenty young officers threw up six who subsequently reached Air rank,[5] including one C.A.S. and two Commanders-in-Chief—not a bad average for one squadron. But we had not nearly enough to keep us busy. Most of the others had been with the squadron a year or so, but I had come straight from No. 1 Flying Training School at Netheravon. When we started that establishment in 1919, under Wing Commander Pip Playfair, it had been impressed on us by Trenchard himself that we were to set a post-war example to the new R.A.F.—to get back to pre-war standards of discipline and smartness on duty and in Mess. On the whole I think we did set a pretty high standard at Netheravon, and it was a bit of a shock to me to find the very different state of affairs in 20 Squadron. Much, of course, was due to the then existing conditions on the Frontier and things improved out of all recognition when we got down to Umballa at the end of the year.

But I'm afraid it must be admitted that discipline was not the strongest suit of our Squadron Commander, an otherwise good officer and a great friend of mine. Shortly after my arrival he departed on long leave, leaving me in command, and I made myself a bit unpopular by a general tightening up of discipline. I also thought it might not be a bad thing to do something

[4] A curious bit of ceremonial consisting of a regular ripple of blank rifle-fire beginning at one flank of the parade and running down the ranks to the other.
[5] They were J. H. S. Tyssen, R. M. Foster, W. A. Staton, L. J. Harvey, L.A. Fiddament and myself.

about the individual ground training of officers, which was virtually non-existent. I had a suspicion, for instance, that the chaps had forgotten most of what they had ever known about their weapons, the Vickers and Lewis guns, and laid on a lecture and demonstration by the Squadron Armament officer on the stripping and reassembling of these weapons—probable causes of stoppage, how to rectify them in the air and so on. I don't say this was a very original or valuable exercise, but it was at least better than hanging about doing nothing, or pottering round a lot of unserviceable aeroplanes, getting in the way of the men who were trying to make them fit to fly. The only place available for this sort of exercise was the "Ante-room" of the Mess—a couple of E.P. tents joined together, with a few rugs on the ground and some rather part-worn sofas and arm-chairs. In the middle of the demonstration when poor Armstrong, the Armament officer, had a Lewis gun in pieces and was holding forth about it to the assembly of rather visibly bored young officers, there was a shattering report from one of the sofas. An officer (one of those, incidentally, who was later to reach Air rank and become a famous Inter-Service and Olympic revolver shot) was practising the art of firing from the hip, the target being a small bird who had rashly decided to attend the demonstration. In the interest of discipline I had to pretend that "We are not amused" (in Queen Victoria's words); the trouble was that actually most of us (except poor old Armstrong) *were* amused; but this sort of attitude to ground training did not tend to make it any easier.

Another characteristic episode which was to have quite unforeseen consequences for me occurred after dinner on a Guest Night, when a couple of tables of bridge were in progress in the aforesaid Ante-room. A certain young officer, who had looked upon the whisky when it was golden, arrived at the conclusion that it was a dull evening and decided to enliven the proceedings by driving a 3-ton Leyland lorry in at the entrance to the Ante-room. The lorry was about four times the size of the entrance and the inevitable result was the collapse of both

E.P. tents on the heads of the bridge players, one of whom was the Colonel of the Cameronians—he from whom I had bought the pony.

Incidentally, a popular pastime which got me into trouble with the Brigadier was shooting with revolvers at the pi-dogs, who admittedly made the nights hideous by their barking and howling. Miscellaneous firing in camp at night is for obvious reasons discouraged on the Frontier. But the repeated notices in Brigade Orders strictly forbidding it were taken as little more than a basis for discussion, until I finally took some drastic and rather brutal action to stop it. All very reprehensible, and I should not like the reader to imagine that these levities represented more than a passing phase in rather special circumstances.

*　　*　　*

Nor should it be thought that this sort of thing was all we had to do in 20 Squadron at Parachinar. We did manage to put in a certain amount of flying—exercises with the Brigade and the Kurram Militia, practice shoots with the Mountain Battery and so on—and an occasional patrol over less settled areas. It can be imagined that we welcomed the odd occasion when something more useful and interesting was required. One day there was an "incident" of some sort nearby in Waziristan. I forget the details, but it was somewhere near Damdil in Mohmit Khel country; a *ghasht* of the Tochi Militia were involved and the Political Agent asked for aircraft to take part in some sort of punitive action. So two old Bristol Fighters of 20 Squadron were detailed to fly to Dardoni (this was before the days of the landing ground at Miranshah, which I was to know so well in later years) at the disposal of the Tochi Scout commander to participate in this operation. We had to anticipate a stay of at least several days at Dardoni, so when I took off from Parachinar that fine, hot afternoon Bristol Fighter 2447 was loaded to the gills: guns, full load of ammunition, bombs on the racks, camera, wireless and a lot of miscellaneous gear like bedding rolls, kitbags, tool box, spare parts and so on, stowed internally or lashed outside. In the gunner's cockpit was another pilot, Flying Officer L. G. Harvey—"Stiffy" Harvey, now retired as an Air Marshal after a distinguished career.

We started by following the road down to Thal. The ancient engines in those first-war vintage aircraft were not very reliable, and when possible (which of course was by no means always) we used to keep within gliding distance of a road; one got into the habit of watching the ground and almost subconsciously "passing oneself on", so to speak, from one spot to another where a forced landing would be anyway less unpleasant than in most places on the Frontier. We then cut across the high, rocky plateau of Spinwam, making for the Tochi road; and at about 3 p.m. were bumbling along at about 3,000 feet just above the haze level, of which the flat surface formed the top of a grey wall around the horizon below the deep blue of a cloudless sky. Visibility down through the dust-haze was poor but one could make out the main features of the country, and I could just distinguish the lighter ribbon of the Tochi road over the port leading edge. It was a lovely afternoon, the engine was running sweetly and Stiffy was drowsing, his face towards the tail and his head just visible over the Scarff gun-ring when I looked round. Then suddenly BANG—a screaming roar from the engine, clouds of steam and gouts of oil flying back and covering the windscreen, very odd things happening to the rev-counter, and B.F. 2447 standing up on her tail! I had the sense to switch off everything and shut off everything else, wound the elevator trimmer right forward and pushed the control stick against the dashboard; and still found to my discomfort that the aircraft was just, but only just, under control, gliding very tail-heavy indeed. It soon dawned on me that the propeller was gone; what I did not realize until later was that the reduction gear had gone with it—the casing sheared almost clean round forward of the holding-on bolts.

I am happy to say that this was not a very usual form of engine failure. Any pilot knows that one of the things one has to be careful about in an aeroplane is the appropriate balance of the load fore and aft of the centre of gravity. I don't know what that reduction gear weighed, but it made up a pretty heavy chunk of metal, fitted as it was with a lot of steel cog-wheels; and its unrehearsed disappearance, together with the propeller, from the extreme forward end inevitably meant that poor old 2447 became almost uncontrollably tail-heavy. There are few less comfortable sensations at the best of times than to be in an aeroplane at the point of stalling and to be unable to do anything about it; this discomfort is accentuated in the very turbulent conditions of hot weather in mountainous country and, though it was not so bad at 3,000 feet, my heart sank at the thought of what it was going to be like when we got down below the level of the surrounding hills.

However, I had descried through the haze what looked to be a relatively flattish bit of ground adjoining the Tochi road, and gingerly turned 2447's nose towards it. A very anxious face appeared over my shoulder; we had no difficulty in talking because, with no engine noise, we were floating in a sort of eerie hush and I told Stiffy to get as much weight forward as he could. So, I perched right forward in the pilot's seat and he leaning forward over the Scarff ring, we glided slowly and groggily down towards the road. As we got lower my fears about the effect of turbulence were fully justified; we were to all intents and purposes out of control, and it was far more by good luck than judgment that we eventually bashed to a grinding standstill—both tyres gone, one Vee of the undercarriage buckled, tail skid wiped off and one bottom plane stove in by a rock.

We were very relieved to feel our feet on hard ground again. But this was tribal country; we had no wish to find ourselves guests of the Wazirs and, thinking it would not be long before they arrived on the scene, considered it undesirable to leave them more removable equipment than we could help—especially ammunition, which was one commodity they were always anxious to acquire. So, loading ourselves up with the Lewis gun and drums, our revolvers, the camera and various odd smaller items, we set off at a smart bustle to cover the three or four hundred stony yards that separated us from the Tochi road where, we thought, we should be less likely to be put in the bag.

We were very lucky to find that flattish bit of ground; and also fortunately it turned out to be only about a mile from the perimeter camp at Idak, which I had failed to notice, being rather fully occupied concentrating on trying to control 2447 and getting her in contact with *terra firma*. Our descent had been observed from Idak and the soldiery had reacted with commendable promptness. Just as we arrived panting and sweating on the road we were relieved to see coming round the corner a couple of armoured cars, followed at the double by a Company of the 2/4th Rajputs who swiftly fanned out and occupied positions covering poor old 2447. What is more, there soon appeared some airmen of our servicing party who happened, at this very appropriate moment, to be passing through Idak on their way by road to Dardoni. So all concerned got down to it, 2447 was fitted with a lashed up jury undercarriage, her tail was tied on an armoured car and what was left of her was towed safely inside the wire at Idak just as darkness fell. A smart bit of work, of which approval was notified by the local peasantry by taking some distant but ineffectual pot-shots at her as she bumped slowly home.

★　★　★

It must have been about a couple of months later that my first tour of duty on the Frontier came to an unexpected and rather uncomfortable end. In that intervening period had occurred the episode of the Leyland lorry in the Ante-room. The young officer concerned had been duly placed under open arrest; and Wing Commander "Ginger" Mitchell, commanding the Frontier Wing with Headquarters at Peshawar, shared my view that as a method of enlivening an hospitable occasion it had not been a very good idea and that, while young officers might be expected to get a bit tight occasionally, this was carrying conviviality to an unacceptable extreme. He decided however to deal with the culprit, not by Court Martial, but by himself dealing with him summarily during a forthcoming visit to the nearest permanent Air Force station at Kohat.

One fine morning, therefore, a little party set off by road for Kohat in the Squadron car, an old open Crossley tourer with a cape-cart hood—also a veteran of France. I sat in front beside the driver, with the reveller and another officer acting as his escort on the back seat. In the course of our journey we came to a place where the road crosses a deep *nullah*, a tributary of the Kurram river; immediately over the bridge the road turns very sharp to the right—on the left a steep sheer wall of rock and on the right the bank of the *nullah* about 50 or 60 feet down at the angle of forty or fifty degrees. The driver took the bridge too fast for the sharp turn on the far side, jerked his wheel over too hard to starboard to avoid hitting the rock wall on the left— and the whole caboodle went over the bank on the right. I have no very clear recollection of what followed: the curious thing was that not only the two officers in the back but the driver (who one would expect to have found it difficult to get out from under the steering wheel) were thrown out on the way down and escaped with minor cuts and bruises. I have a vague memory of trying to scramble out over the top of the side door as the car rolled over sideways several times and finished upside down in the stony bed of the *nullah* with me pinned half out, half in, by the top of the side door across my knees. Fortunately the *nullah* was dry: after a storm it would be a raging torrent.

It was a painful experience. The car was too heavy for my three companions to move and I lay there face down in the rocks of the nullah-bed for something like half an hour, with the rather sharp side of a heavy staff car across my crossed knees. Eventually some Pathans came along the road driving camels; between them they managed to lift the car enough to pull me out, and I was carried to a nearby Militia picquet to await an ambulance, and then on to hospital in Kohat.

★   ★   ★

When I emerged after some hot and uncomfortable weeks, 20 Squadron was packing up to move to Umballa, the big cantonment in the Punjab where Kim, hidden in Colonel Creighton's garden, had overheard the *Jang-i-Lat* Sahib issuing the orders for that Frontier war. It was a pleasant "family" station where the R.A.F. had taken over the old British Cavalry mess, and we had decent barracks and a good airfield—though still not enough flying to be good for us. There was polo and tennis and some not very good shooting, and diversions like a cricket week at Patiala where Hirst and Rhodes played very gently against us for the Maharajah's XI. And during the following hot weather I proved myself as physically tough as my father by surviving—much to everyone's surprise—a combination of pleurisy and an assortment of other unglamorous Oriental diseases which, however, resulted in my being sent home prematurely, long before the expiry of the normal five-year tour overseas.

8   Conky: India, 1922

Conky, as the late Colonel Sir John F. Turner was affectionately
known to a host of friends, was a rich character on the polo
ground; he was a rich character anywhere, come to that, but it
was when playing polo that he was seen at his best. Stocky and
verging on the portly, with a strong beak of a nose set in a face
of seamed oak, his irreverent Rabelaisian humour and the laugh
always bubbling near the surface more than made up for any lack
of resemblance to Gary Cooper or Victor Mature. He was no
oil-painting, was Conky, but a grand chap and a first-rate sapper.

In Kitchener's day Umballa was the scene of some of the best
polo tournaments in India. But by the early 'twenties the
Dharmsala earthquake had changed the course of the underground stream that watered what had been a big cavalry station.
The consequent shortage of water not only banished all but one
regiment of Indian cavalry, but turned the formerly lovely polo
ground into a parched expanse of dry *dhoob* grass. The mice
liked the roots of that *dhoob* grass, and their tunnelling operations were regarded as a bit of a menace. I do not actually remember any broken fetlocks as a result; but we tried all sorts of
experiments to liquidate the mice. "Liquidate" was the right
word for one such—not very successful. The tip of a hose from
an old byle-drawn water-cart was poked into one hole, while
an expectant circle of chaps with terriers and sawn-off polo
sticks waited for the dripping mice to pop out of the others.
There was an occasional wild flurry, with much yapping of
excited terriers, and a good time was had by all. But the death-
rate among the mice was not very high.

We watered those grounds on special occasions as best we
could. But, especially in the hot weather before the monsoon
broke, the players were mostly dimly-seen shapes in a rapidly

moving cloud of dust, from the midst of which a stream of cheerfully picturesque invective identified Conky, in a huge, quilted Cawnpore topi, riding sixteen annas, with his short legs going like flails on his pony's sweating flanks. He was perhaps not quite Hurlingham or Meadowbrook form, but a pretty effective performer—and anyway one never had a dull moment when he was on the ground.

I only once remember Conky being strangely silent on the polo ground. It happened this way. He had come to Umballa from the Frontier, where he had been a garrison engineer in Waziristan and had seen two of his companions at the bridge table shot down by a Mahsud sepoy, when a Frontier Irregular Corps mutinied and turned on their officers. He shared a bungalow with the Wing Commander (now Air Chief Marshal Sir Christopher Courtney), and 20 Squadron took him to their bosoms.

It so happened that about that time, many years ago, it was decided to create a new appointment of Chief Engineer for the R.A.F. in India, to build us the barracks and hangars which, of course, had not existed before the Kaiser's war, and to make the chain of airfields on the strategic route to Singapore—Mingaladon, Mergui and Victoria Point, names now familiar to so many who fought in S.E.A.C. in that later war then undreamt of. Conky thought this was just his cup of tea—and so did we of the R.A.F. But he had a rival, who had the advantage that he was serving on the Staff in Delhi and Simla and was thus better able, by divers means, to keep his own existence and qualifications before the notice of the Great and (or anyway so we thought, no doubt quite unjustly) to slip the odd spoke into the wheel of any rival candidate for the job. And lo! in due course there arrived from On High instructions to the effect that Lieut.-Colonel Turner was to report forthwith to somewhere on the Frontier, as C.R.E. of a column that was about to go in to cover the construction of a road and establish what was later to become the great fortified camp at Razmak, in the heart of Waziristan.

The occasion obviously called for guile. The rival had taken the first trick. Moreover the following Monday was the first day of Umballa week, with its usual frivolities, a race-meeting and the Umballa autumn tournament in which Conky was, on somewhat tenuous grounds (mainly, as far as I remember, because he shared that bungalow with the Wing Commander), playing for a R.A.F. team. The inevitable Irish Medical Officer was a keen polo-player—as a matter of fact he was the polo secretary at Umballa that year. And a regretful signal was despatched to say that most unfortunately Lieut.-Colonel Turner was seriously ill with a bad attack of malaria and was very unlikely to be fit to take over this important appointment in the near future. Second trick to Conky.

Came the first day of the tournament and the R.A.F. were playing the Royal Fusiliers from Jullundur, a goodish team who had the advantage of being trained by their Colonel, who had been a member of de Lisle's famous Durham Light Infantry side in former years. At first Conky was very much in evidence, galloping furiously up and down the ground and counselling his side in a hoarse voice and the usual colourful terms. But while he was changing ponies after the first chukker a kind friend sought him out. "Look here, old boy," he said, anxiously confidential, "I don't quite know what you can do about it, but old So-and-So is in the Stand." Old So-and-So was the Engineer in Chief from Army Headquarters, who no doubt had been thinking kindly that after the game he really must go and see poor Conky on his sick bed. Well—there was obviously nothing to be done about it. He couldn't possibly run out at that stage. But for the rest of that match an eerie hush descended upon Conky; the enormous topi was crammed hard down over his nose and he kept as much as possible on the far side of the game to the Stand.

It took a Conky to get away with that one. But he did. He got the job with the R.A.F. in India; he built our workshops and hangars and laid out our new airfields. What is more, he went on to become the head of all R.A.F. Works, and was responsible for many excellent R.A.F. stations that were built in this country in the years before Hitler's war.

9   When Soldiering Was Really
Soldiering: Aldershot, 1925–1928

"Well, George, now we're back home I suppose you and me will be able to resume command of our Companies." Thus, one of a couple of Company Sergeant-Majors leaning on the rail of a troopship bringing a Guards battalion home from Egypt, as she was warped alongside the quay at Tilbury one far-off day between the wars. How right he was.

This is not to suggest for one moment that he found his officers anything but admirable; but from long experience he was aware that, once the battalion was back at Wellington Barracks or Chelsea, Windsor or Pirbright, they would once more devote an appropriate proportion of their time and energies to hunting and shooting, racing and polo and the many other agreeable occupations which in those days enabled officers of the Brigade of Guards, in their zeal for the Service, to extend to their Warrant and Non-commissioned officers such prolonged and valuable opportunities for the exercise of responsibility.

Was there not the story of one of those splendid pre-war Company Sergeant-Majors of Foot Guards, initiating a recruit into the glories of the battalion that had done him the honour of receiving him into its ranks: "Yer Comp'ny Commander," he was overheard to say, perfectly seriously, in a parade-ground voice, "is Captain the Honourable So-and-So. One of these days I hopes to have the honour of pointing 'im out to you."

It is true that the officers did manage to fit in a bit of soldiering in the late summers when the 4th Guards Brigade used to descend from London to join the two Line Brigades of the

Second Division for collective training. When they did so, they did it very well. They were admirably trained and no one could accuse them of being stale; they were not afraid of responsibility nor slow to take the initiative; they were kind to and had a pleasant, easy way with Very Senior Officers; and their pursuit of the aforesaid agreeable occupations had endowed most of them with a nice eye for country. In fact, they were good soldiers.

In those palmy days of the 'twenties it was my good fortune to command No. 4 Squadron of the Royal Air Force, which trained with the Second Division at Aldershot. Driving back from near Guildford to Somerset the other day I passed through a stretch of country which brought back to my mind nostalgic memories of that pleasant, easy-going, somehow agreeably amateur soldiering of thirty years ago.[1]

A distant view of Chobham Ridges where, in the grey dawn of a summer morning, a demonstration of an experimental and slightly Heath-Robinsonian anti-tank obstacle was honoured by the presence—amongst many others—of Roger, tall and resplendent in Blues cloak and brass-bound cap (donned, dare I suggest, hastily over white waistcoat and tails which he had not had time to change); and the *sotto voce* comment of a somewhat rumpled rifleman, one of the recumbent garrison of that "Forward Defended Locality", who had spent the night in the heather, "Oo's this (concupiscent) Cossack?"

That bend in the road among the trees as one comes down from the Hog's Back towards Farnham; a long column of horsed artillery halted in the late dusk, the gunners dismounted and gossiping, bandoliers like polished mahogany, puttees neatly rolled with the tapes above the ankles, flat khaki caps on their heads and steel helmets slung to the shoulder by the chin-straps, the drivers with that heavy leather shield strapped to the right leg; "Put those cigarettes out there" as an "enemy" aeroplane bumbled overhead.

A long, straight stretch of road near Alton and a cheerful

[1] This was written in 1956.

marching column, the men in shirt-sleeves as the day was warm, the Brigade-Major trotting busily up the column on his horse; he was a first-rate soldier but he was the most—well, shall we say that his Maker had not adorned him with the features of an Adonis. A little Cockney soldier in the perspiring column of fours (yes, fours in those days), tin hat tipped over his eyebrows, rifle slung butt-upwards to his shoulder, a grass stalk between his teeth, summed up the situation as the Brigade-Major bustled by: "Ah well," he said, very philosophically, "I'd rather 'ave my face walkin' than 'is ridin'."

Manœuvres were usually rather fun—anyway when the weather did not let us down as it did (was it in 1927?) when the Aldershot Divisions went to train in Oxfordshire and the 4th Guards Brigade rashly decided on Gipsy Bottom as the site for their camp. I, knowing what the Bicester Thursday country could ride like in a wet season, chose for my camp a field on Sam Ashton's farm at Scotsgrove with a steepish slope down to the River Thame. The site was consequently (I admit only relatively) well drained—though as an aerodrome it made my pilots suck their teeth a bit when they first had to get the old Bristol Fighters into it.

Even that year one managed to combine a bit of pleasure with business; a morning's cubbing in Waterperry Wood before zero hour, or digging out a badger with old George Baker, the South Oxfordshire huntsman, between battles.

The doughty and rather frosty-faced old warrior who then commanded the Second Division was air-minded for his generation. And his modernity frequently took the not always very welcome form of insisting on my accompanying him in the ancient dark-green motor car in which he used to drive himself round the battlefields. One evening, for instance, during the 4th Guards Brigade training, he said as he went up to bed in the "Wellington Arms" at Stratfield Turgis, "We'll go and see them force the crossing of the Loddon at dawn—you'd better get yourself into the picture and be ready at 04.30." Now, I do not like getting up before dawn, even a pearly

August dawn in Hampshire. But at about 05.00 hours we drove up to a bridge which was by way of being held by a troop of Household Cavalry, I with my Aldershot Command 1-inch map duly marked.

It was a lovely, peaceful scene as the sun rose on a perfect morning—a lark singing, cows hock-deep in flowery grass and, under wisps of mist rising off the river, concentric rings where a trout had punished an inexperienced March Brown for being such a fool as to be up before dawn. From the far bank ominous sounds broke upon the morning calm—rattle of rifle fire from down-stream, boom from a blank round of 18-pounder, rumble of tank engines in the distance. On this side of the bridge a trooper lay on his tummy in the grass by the road, his rifle at his elbow; on the other side of the road was a little yellow flag, the anti-tank gun of the 'twenties.

I experienced a somewhat sinking feeling and, to keep my courage up, said wishfully, "Well, this is a *jolly* good show, the chaps really *are* learning at last to take cover from the air—hardly a sign of them anywhere." But Peter Strickland's face was a shade more frosty than usual as he swung the old car round to go up the lane to the farm-house where the troop H.Q. was supposed to be. Sure enough, there in the yard were black horses and a few troopers *and* a smart chauffeur with cockaded cap standing by a very long, sleek, black limousine on the back seat of which was to be seen an enormous hamper.

Old Peter thrust his lean face out at the man and, in a voice like the rasp of a file, inquired, "What do you think you're doing here?" The poor chauffeur was nonplussed. "I'm er—I've er—I've brought his Lordship's breakfast, Sir." His Lordship, commanding the troop, was still conserving his energy in a very comfortable bed upstairs. After all, Cardigan never dreamt of getting up at that unearthly hour, even on the morning of Balaclava.

I prefer to draw a veil over the atomic explosion that followed. But I'm afraid I could not bring myself even to try to persuade the General that this was but another example of the thoughtful attention habitually devoted by officers of His Majesty's Household Troops (with such rewarding results) to training their non-commissioned officers by giving them opportunities to exercise command.

10   A Name on a Bullet:
North-West Frontier, 1936

There are a few people—I think very few—who are genuinely unafraid in war; they are mostly men with no imagination and therefore not really the bravest, or indeed the best soldiers. There are more who are afraid like the rest of us, but have the self-control and real courage to overcome their fears to a degree that enables them repeatedly to perform prodigies of valour; to some of these danger is liable to become something almost in the nature of a drug, and on them the wise commander will keep a watchful eye, easing them off before they crack up—if they have not got themselves killed first. There are many who in their inmost hearts are terrified until "the burning moment breaks and all things else are out of mind"[1]—that moment when the barrage lifts or the flak comes up over the target. There are some who simply lack the moral fibre to face danger at all—and the surprising thing to me is not that they are so many, but so few; it is sometimes necessary to make an example of the real skrimshanker, but to the unhappy weakling we are now more understanding and humane than we were in my young days. For the most part, however, men in battle are afraid and at the same time ordinarily brave in an unspectacular way—not courting death but not trying to dodge it, doing their duty under fire with resignation and dogged courage, though seldom in real life with the cheerful bravado beloved of certain brands of popular fiction.

But just once in a way in war one comes across the unfortunate individual (and I'm not sure he isn't the bravest of all) to whom suddenly the premonition of death comes with absolute

[1] *Into Battle* by Julian Grenfell.

and unquestioned certainty. Most of us are endowed with a sort of protective psychological armour; others will get shot down, or brewed-up in their tank or riddled with machine-gun bullets—but not I; I shall be all right, I shall come through and live to tell the tale. Now I come to think of it, that sort of in-stinctive feeling applies also to natural disasters; other people will be killed by tornadoes or drowned by tidal waves but not we ourselves—we shall read about them in the papers next day. I remember the reactions of Hermione and myself when we had been knocked about by our bungalow falling in on us in the great earthquake at Quetta, almost of incredulity; this had actually happened to US! There were moments under that hot and dusty pile of bricks when I thought—Well, this is it—until I saw a tiny gleam from a hurricane lamp and knew that where light could get in, air could, so I was not going to be suffocated after all, as so many of my poor airmen were. We got away with it, unlike the thousands of poor devils in similar circum-stances who did not; so the protective armour remained—was, perhaps, even strengthened.

I suppose the same sort of thing is true of the ordinary hazards of motoring; if it were not, perhaps the toll of death on our roads would be less appalling.

Anyway, there are the ill-starred few who lack that protec-tive armour, or on whom it suddenly melts; to them comes the knowledge—they do not just think or fear, they know—that in a coming battle there will be a bullet or a shell with their name on it. And this happens not only in a great war. Many years ago I had first-hand experience of a striking case of it, which occur-red in a little tribal affair of a kind that was almost an annual event on the North-West Frontier in the old days.

★   ★   ★

One evening in the late autumn of 1936 the Brigadier com-manding the Rawalpindi Brigade gave a little drink party. Cyril Noyes and his beautiful wife Vi were old friends of ours from Quetta days, and I was commanding 3 (Indian) Wing of the R.A.F. with headquarters at 'Pindi; so we were at the party, together with the other commanding officers on the Station and their wives—Infantry, Gunners, Sappers and Signalmen—the District Commissioner, the head policeman and so on. When the cheerful noise was at its height (why is it that everyone on these social occasions seems to find it necessary to talk at the tops of their voices?), a Sikh orderly made his presence on the veranda known by the usual clearing of the throat. He was the bearer of a signal to the effect that there had been an "incident" in the Khaisora valley in Waziristan; the Bannu Brigade had been rather nastily mauled in an ambush by Madi Khel and Tori Khel Wazirs under a turbulent priest called the Fakir of Ipi; a punitive expedition was to be laid on; and the 'Pindi Brigade and my Wing were to proceed at once to join up with the Razmak Brigade on the Frontier.

Well—that was all very agreeable as far as we were concerned; it was the sort of thing that every right-minded soldier hoped for. The party was coming to an end anyway, and we all drifted off to warn our units to get ready to move at short notice.

But it so happened that one of the battalion commanders, Aubrey Mansfield[2] of the 1/35th Punjab Regiment, and his wife Sophie were staying at the time with the Noyeses in their large and comfortable official bungalow; the young wife was the daughter of an old friend of Vi's, and was expecting her first baby in about a couple of months' time. That night, when Cyril went up to bed, Aubrey detained Vi in the drawing-room and—standing by the fire with a half-finished whisky and soda in his hand—told her in a flat, matter-of-fact voice that he was not coming back from this show in Waziristan and he wanted to discuss with her a *bundobast*[3] for the care of his wife—or rather widow, though I don't suppose he used the word.

---

[2] The names of this character and his Regiment are fictitious; otherwise the story is true; though I cannot trust my memory to be absolutely accurate in matters of detail.

[3] Arrangement.

It can be imagined that this was a pretty difficult facer even for so wise and experienced a woman as Vi. He was not drunk —she knew he never drank to excess; a lean, hard-bitten, very fit-looking chap with a good fighting record, he was the last man to suffer from emotional delusions. Poor Vi protested rather feebly, told him not to be ridiculous—this was just one of those little Frontier shows of which he had been in several before—of *course* he'd come back—what on earth did he think he was talking about?—and so on. But he was unmoved, pragmatic and definite—said he knew he was going to be killed, it could not be helped, and she must make the arrangements for Sophie to go home and have the baby in the care of her parents in Ireland.

And a day or two later, when Hermione went with Vi to see the battalion off at the station (I had already gone by air to the Frontier), Aubrey took Vi by the arm and led her to the end of the platform to tell her again that she must take this seriously, and that he relied on her to see that the proper arrangements were made for Sophie and the baby.

*   *   *

Some weeks passed before I was to connect with the 'Pindi Brigade again; and I must now tell briefly the story of the opening stages of this very typical little Frontier campaign.

One of the basic principles of Frontier policy was to open up that wild country by the construction of roads—the same technique by which General Wade had brought under control the tribal areas of Scotland a couple of centuries before. For this purpose the initial striking force—consisting of the Razmak Brigade with attached artillery and Sappers, and a company of light tanks from Peshawar—was concentrated at Mirali, a fortified cantonment on the Tochi road. Their job was to cover the construction of the new road forward into the Khaisora and Shaktu valleys and, in dealing with the opposition we knew would be encountered, to teach the tribesmen who had attacked the Bannu Brigade in November that they could not indulge with impunity in their favourite pastime of being beastly to the Indian Army.

The first move was to advance into tribal territory and establish a strong perimeter camp on the Jaler Algad, a tributary of the Khaisora river. Thence Khaicol, as it was called, sallied forth daily to cover the road building, to blow up fighting towers[4] and the houses of tribal leaders, including the Fakir's country cottage among the apricot groves of Zarinai—and generally to indulge in mildly provocative martial exercises with the object of inducing the Wazir to fight. In this we sometimes succeeded and a good time was had by all, including the enemy—the casualties were not very serious on either side.

Meanwhile the 'Pindi Brigade was relegated to the necessary but unglamorous role of road protection—picqueting the heights between Mirali and Jaler to cover the supply traffic using that stretch of track. This meant that Mansfield's premonition seemed less than ever likely to be realized.

* * *

I thought at the time, and still think, that the situation could have been dealt with just as effectively and a good deal less expensively by leaving it to the R.A.F.—to the method known as Air Control which we had proved time and again could be effectively applied in these conditions. However, the Powers that were in Delhi had decided that troops were to be employed —and there was something to be said for it in this case. That being so, I was determined that the Air Force should be used to support them on sensible lines. I had long been making myself a nuisance to my betters on the subject of what I regarded as the unimaginative system of training for Army/Air co-operation on the Frontier. I was sure that ordinary air reconnaissance on the Aldershot Command model of the day was useless in mountain warfare—one simply cannot see, except occasionally by sheer luck, a skilled tribal enemy who does not want to be

[4] Towers two or three storeys high with slits for rifles—not unlike the keeps of early Scottish castles.

seen in that rugged, scrub-covered terrain. I was equally convinced that the Air could be very useful as a means of affording
quick, close fire support; the Pathan disliked being attacked
from the air, which deprived him of his prized inaccessibility.
So it was not a matter (as in more "civilized" warfare) of the
airman telling the soldier where the enemy was, but the other
way round—the soldier, who is being shot at, must tell the airman where opposition is coming from, and his job is then to
blast it out of the way by bombing and machine-gun fire. I had
enjoyed argument on this subject the year before at Quetta
with Colonel Montgomery, then a teacher at the Staff College,
where the old methods were still being taught—Monty's lack
of any practical experience of Frontier warfare did not inhibit
him from holding strong views about it; to be honest, my own
experience was not much more than his, but was enough to
convince me that I was right.

Fortunately Cyril Noyes agreed with me[5] and between us
we had succeeded in persuading our superiors, only a couple of
months before, to allow us to conduct a period of special training and trials by the 'Pindi Brigade and my Wing in the hills
behind Taxila. The result had been to convince us of the valid-
ity of our theories. And now, almost immediately afterwards,
here we were—or anyway here I was with my Wing—given
the opportunity of putting those theories into practice with ball
ammunition instead of blank. All great fun—and it worked.
The jolly old Cavalry General who had said to me at the Commanding Officers' conference before the move to Jaler, "Now
then, young feller, can't have you breakin' up the coveys you
know," later found that in fact we had rather spoilt his shootin'
—though I don't think his subordinate commanders viewed
that as a matter for regret.

My two squadrons, 5 and 20[6] were based at Miranshah at the
head of the Tochi valley. But an essential feature of our system

---

[5] So also did my A.O.C., Air Marshal Ludlow-Hewitt.

[6] Oddly enough I had served as a Flight Commander in both these squadrons
in days gone by.

was that if the Air Force Commander was to be any good he must be on the ground, as far forward as he could get, so that he could see what was going on, be in close personal contact with the Force commander and thus be able to bring his fire down quickly when and where it was needed—the essence of effective support was *speedy* action. So there I was alongside John Marshall, commanding Khaicol, on a Militia pony attended by an amiable Afridi horse-holder from the Tochi Scouts, his beard dyed orange with henna. My little mobile headquarters comprised a cheerful Gunner Captain as operations adjutant, a bundle of white oil-cloth strips for passing short coded messages to the air (no luxuries like R/T in India in those days), a very inefficient wireless set and a mule-borne field telephone back to the squadrons at Miranshah—oddly enough, the line was never cut by the Wazirs, as I was assured it would be.

Thus I have two tenuous claims to distinction; one that I was the first man to intercept (albeit quite ineffectively) an enemy aircraft over England; the other that I am the only Air Force commander to have gone to war on a horse!

*   *   *

In this enjoyable and not very hazardous sort of campaigning the first weeks of December passed all too quickly. Incidentally, we were not bothered with newspapers up in the Khaisora, and I had occasion, some twenty years later in New York, to tell the Duke of Windsor that I was probably the first man with whom he had talked who had not known about the abdication until some ten days after the event. Shortly before Christmas it looked as though the back of the job had been broken; there were indications that a little more pressure would be enough to persuade the enemy to throw in the sponge and send representatives to a *Jirga*[7] to discuss terms. So a final operation was laid on. The two Brigades joined forces at Jaler; the Razmak

[7] Meeting—conference with the Military commander and the Political Agent.

Brigade was to go straight through up the Khaisora to Damdil
on the Central Waziristan road, and thence on back to barracks; the 'Pindi Brigade would cover its passage, destroy a
village called Dakai Kalai, the home of a specially dissident section of Tori Khel Wazirs, and be back in Jaler by nightfall.
There was a golden rule of Frontier warfare—never get caught
out in the open at night, but always get back to the cover of a
prepared perimeter camp with its *sangars*[8] and shelter pits
against the sniper that snipeth by night.

The main job that day being for the 'Pindi Brigade, I had
attached my little headquarters to theirs; and at 4 a.m. on the
22nd was standing by Gate C, the southern exit to Jaler Camp,
with Cyril and his Brigade Major, McDonald, who had been at
Camberley with me two or three years before, and Jogie
Crichton the Political Agent, amid a silent and rather sleepy
knot of men and loaded mules—a vast cold sky ablaze with
stars, not a breath of wind and a strong smell of incinerator
smoke, as the advance guard moved out and away into the
darkness across the slope marked on the map "stony waste"
towards the Khaisora. The shuffle and tramp of men's boots in
the dust; a harness chain jingling, a mule kicking and squealing; pi-dogs barking in the far distance. A horse blew through
his nostrils and a low voice said, "That bloody battery is late,
George—where the hell are they?"

I propped myself against a *sangar* wall in a little hollow below
the level of the track and watched the upper half of men and
mules go by looming against the stars. The Brigade Major,
silent and stolid by the gate, flashed an electric torch occasionally at his wrist watch. The 2/11th Sikhs, the old 15th Ludhiana
Sikhs, went by—tightly rolled turbans and bearded profiles—
their second-in-command "Tiny" Farwell (an enormous man,
needless to say) blotting out half the starlight as he strode past;
and, in the nick of time, that battery—big mules with sections
of mountain howitzers or ammunition *Yakdans*[9] on their backs,

[8] Rough stone walls.
[9] Big leather ammunition containers, two to a mule.

the domed helmets of British gunners, and the battery commander with his Survey section on horse-back.

I yawned cavernously and audibly—I'm never at my best at four in the morning. "Come on now," said Cyril suddenly, "off we go—wake up Jack"; and we were away through the gap in the wall into the night.

★   ★   ★

At noon we were on a little shelf on the western slope of a hillock overlooking the Khaisora—a wide expanse of white stones among which trickles of shallow water reflected the sky. A pennon fluttering below the tip of a lance jammed between two boulders marked Brigade headquarters, where we sat eating our sandwiches and drinking coffee from a thermos. Two or three hundred yards across the river-bed was Dakai Kalai, a huddle of brown hovels with a fighting tower or two, at the foot of a hill shaped like a huge barracked[10] camel (Hampshire ridge we called it at the time) its flanks dotted with sparse scrub like the tufts of fur on the camel's tawny hide. Scattered here and there along the river banks were green patches of cultivation, little groves of fruit trees and the occasional mud hut. And away to the left was Hill 2136, a tangle of arid uplands scarred by ravines of which the beds were still in deep shadow while the sun threw dark silhouettes of mountain and crag on to their southern slopes. That was the battalion area of the 1/35th Punjabis who had occupied it—as the Hampshires had the hill beyond Dakai Kalai—against only slight opposition. The 2/11th Sikhs were in reserve in the river-bed, and the big black Madrassi Sappers and Miners were busy preparing the demolitions in the village itself.

Everything so far had gone rather uneventfully according to plan, so much so that one rather wondered—it was not like the Wazir to take it so tamely. There had been one or two minor encounters, but nothing of any significance. The Razmak Brigade had gone through—the tail of their rearguard could still be seen, an orderly disorder of men and mules in the valley

[10] The position of a camel at rest, with his legs folded under him.

to the right of Dakai Kalai. A helio winked from Hill 2136; from behind us came the occasional "Bang" of a pack howitzer —the flutter of the shell overhead and the "Crrrump" as it burst out of sight beyond the Khaisora. A camel *Kajawah*[11] made its undulating way back with a wounded man. Above the hills to the westward, where Shuedar raised its rampart of snow against a sky of cloudless blue, a couple of aircraft bumbled round, the distant throaty drone of their engines filling the warm air. And from time to time an old Wapiti[12] would slant steeply down, throttled back, into the valley towards us, the gunner's arm raised ready to throw the message bag with black —yellow—red streamers, containing scraps of information.

The whole plan was on a pre-arranged programme timed to ensure that we should be back in Jaler Camp by the time it got dark at about 6 p.m. I was sitting on my boulder in the sun, field-glasses focused on Dakai Kalai when, exactly at the scheduled moment, a sapper across the river threw his weight on to the ratchet of an exploder. A sudden flat wave of dust shot out in a circle round the base of the nearest fighting tower, which crumbled slowly in on itself into a thick ball of brown dust and smoke. Half a dozen frightened pigeons orbited above the dust-cloud as the muffled "Boom" of the explosion floated across on the still air, followed by a second and a third as other towers dissolved into piles of stinking *mutti*[13] and broken rafters. Then men were seen moving among the brown, flat-roofed houses and from one after another wisps of white smoke arose, soon to form a slowly drifting curtain northwards across the valley.

In a few minutes the job was completed and the Sappers left the devastated village, dropping down the bank into the river-bed and splashing through shallow runnels as they came away; in that crystal clear air I could see little puffs of blue smoke as

[11] A primitive form of ambulance—a saddle fitted with two stretchers, one each side of the hump.
[12] A very useful two-seater aeroplane of the day.
[13] Mud mixed with chopped straw.

the tall Sapper Major paused to light his pipe before trudging after his men.

*   *   *

The withdrawal was timed to begin at 12.30—and at 12.30 it duly began. Three aircraft were following one another in a wide circuit over beyond Hampshire ridge and the 2136 feature. There was a hoarse roar of exhausts as a section of light tanks lurched forward out of a clump of fruit trees near Dakai Kalai, and halted by a strip of cultivation two or three hundred yards up the bank of the *nullah* to the left of the village. Then little figures of men and the white flutter of a picquet strip[14] were seen moving down the hill beyond, as the forward platoons came away. I could see a Company of Sikhs fanning out across the river-bed and a section of their machine guns on the bluff to our right, ready to cover the Hampshires' withdrawal. And soon afterwards we of Force H.Q. left our shelf and clambered down into the river-bed, ready to move back ourselves when the right moment came. "Well," said Brownlow, the Gunner Major, "touch wood—all seems to be going very nicely."

And almost as he said it, things began to happen rather rapidly.

The guns behind us were putting over salvo after salvo to cover the withdrawal—their echoes reverberating from hill to steep hill in that hollow country, the flutter of their shells like pigeons' wings overhead. An aircraft dropped a message on us reporting picquets coming away, but only minor enemy movement. Then suddenly a clangour of small-arms fire broke out to south-west of us—the sustained, irregular thump of rifles and stammering of automatic weapons. An agitated helio flashed from 2136, and there was a hammering noise like that of riveters in a ship-yard as the tanks opened fire. The epicentre of the confused din seemed to be at the western end of the 2136 feature and the southern slopes of Hampshire ridge. A red Verey

---

[14] When a picquet left its position, one man trailed a white calico strip so that the Air could see they were coming away.

light soared and a smoke-candle threw up a billow of white cloud beyond the sky-line. Another salvo crashed from the little howitzers, and another; and at that moment first one aircraft and then another dipped into a shallow dive and the "Crrrump" of bombs added to the pandemonium, thickening the surge of smoke and dust that rose from beyond the crest— again the lunatic hammering of the tank guns from the *nullah* bank.

What was happening was a typical example of the dangerously clever tactics of the Pathan—the sudden deadly rush at the most vulnerable moment of withdrawal had struck a forward Company of the 1/35th just as they started coming away. The communications with battalions were bad—the field wireless sets of those days were pretty indifferent; and for the moment there was some confusion and uncertainty down there in the river-bed. But Cyril quickly decided to put in a counter-attack by the 2/11th Sikhs to relieve pressure on the Punjabis— actually, as it turned out, that was not really necessary; the 1/35th were a good battalion and were able to handle the situation for themselves. We stayed where we were while the counter-attack was being staged—I called up additional aircraft from Miranshah to cover and support it. But it soon became obvious that there was not a hope of getting the Brigade back into Jaler before dark. And while waiting we learnt from a message by runner that Aubrey Mansfield, in his command post on the ridge, hearing the sudden clatter to his left had raised his field-glasses to see what was happening—and a bullet hit him between the eyes, killing him instantly.

* * *

Well—we did not get back to Jaler by nightfall. I have given elsewhere[15] an account of what did happen, and to round off the story will repeat some of it here:

Fortunately there was an old and rather part-worn perimeter camp-site with sangars and some trenches, at Biche Kaskai a few

[15] See *The Central Blue,*' pages 135–6.

miles down the valley opposite the remains of Zarinai, and we got back there just as night was falling. The sangars and pits gave welcome protection against the sniping that went on all night but, of course, our rations and—what was more—our greatcoats and blankets were back at Jaler. I have very seldom been so cold. Waziristan in December could be pretty cold at night and was no place to spend a night in the open with nothing on but shirts and shorts[16] —we could light no fires because of the snipers.

It was an uncomfortable but in retrospect a funny night. One's natural discomfort owing to the cold and lack of food and drink was not ameliorated by the constant sniping which, while not dangerous in itself, caused the occasional mule to break loose from his pickets and gallivant about inside the perimeter, which I found most alarming. Cyril Noyes, McDonald and I wedged ourselves into a sort of little grave about three feet deep which just held us, packed like sardines, and gave us protection.

There would be a crack and the whine of a sniper's bullet, a squeal and the sound of galloping hoofs and jingling harness-chains and objurgations from all sides in Urdu and the tongue of Hampshire— —I lay in constant terror of finding a large mule's hoof in my eye. Indeed at about two o'clock in the morning I was awakened by a shower of dust and small stones and looked up to see against the frosty moon the head and huge ears of a battery mule, pulled up just in time to avoid our prostrate forms. However, "even the weariest river winds somewhere safe to sea" and with the dawn came the welcome sun, which soon warmed us up as we tramped back to breakfast across the stony levels to Jaler.

Actually that was not quite all that happened that night. At about nine o'clock Cyril, cramped and cold in that dusty little pit, said, "You know, I'm awfully worried about Vi—and Sophie. I'd hate them to hear about this first from the newspaper." (The short casualty list had gone back by wireless to Mirali.) I bethought me of my little D.3 field telephone. The only land-line we had, it was not a very efficient instrument even at short range, and it was the longest of long odds against being able to connect through Mirali with the ordinary Posts

[16] Actually I'm afraid this was rather shooting a line—we did have cardigans.

and Telegraphs system back across the Indus to Rawalpindi. But it seemed worth having a try—and it came off; in under half-an-hour there at the other end was Vi—in Cyril's study at home. Said he from his hole in the ground, "Listen, I'm afraid I've got very bad news for you—Aubrey—" Vi interrupted him; "I know," she said, "we know—no no, Sophie just knew as soon as it happened." No one had told them; but the knowledge had come to her with the same certainty that the fore-knowledge had come to him.

* * *

So that is my true story of a name on a bullet. "There are more things in heaven and earth Horatio . . ." And let no one tell me that there is no such thing as genuine premonition.

"Stock!" said my father-in-law. "Stock! You mean hunting tie." He was a stickler in these matters. He was always beautifully turned out, though the cut of his coat and boots looked a little old-fashioned to me. He was a grand man to hounds. But he had a "thing" about certain words. There was, for instance, no such thing as a hunting crop; one carried a whip. And though others might hunt in pink, my father-in-law's rather long-skirted, high-buttoned coat was red.

My mother-in-law was no less meticulous, but perhaps a little kinder. Those were days before I aspired to a pink coat. But my mother-in-law on the whole approved of my black coat, twill breeches and modest patent-leather tops. She had, however, a "thing" about pins. One did not wear a short pin with a fox's head in one's tie. I must have a rather long, plain gold pin, worn, of course, horizontal—on no account vertical; that was almost the mark of the beast. She would give me one. And she did. And my little fox's head, of which I was secretly rather proud, was quietly banished.

*   *   *

That was in the early carefree twenties, and Pin has since been my inseparable companion until last autumn, when the worst happened. We had been carrying the corn, I myself driving the tractor. When we got home I found Pin was gone from my tie.

I really mourn Pin. He had been with me through two wars —one big and one little one. He had travelled with me, keeping my tie in place, in uniform and plain clothes, over most of the world, by air and sea. But his especial virtue was his capacity to bring back to my mind some of the happiest moments of my life—in the hunting field, by Dorset trout streams, by Scottish

sea lochs, by the tumbling rivers of Kashmir and by quiet snipe
jheels in the diamond-clear mornings of Indian winters.

He was particularly helpful in untangling knots in casts.
During my last leave he did that, on the bank of the tidal beat
of a little river in Mull, with the curlew crying, and the hills of
Morven blue against a cloudy September sky. It was one of
those golden afternoons, with hardly a breath of wind, which
are so rewarding between the rains of the Western Isles—obviously not a day for the little wet Peter Ross or Grouse and
Claret which had been taking some nice sea-trout in the Bridge
pool during preceding days of wind and rain. But a small dark
spinner fished dry had already produced three fish, one a nice
estuary trout of $1\frac{3}{4}$ pounds, foul-hooked in the eyelid (if a trout
can be said to have an eyelid). Then there was a nice fish moving
in the fast deep water right under the far bank above the bridge
—a very long cast with the fly coming back to one quickly.
About the third or fourth cast I made a mess of it; felt the shock
as the cast fouled the line behind my shoulder; and back she
came with one of those inexplicable tangles which the fisherman's Gremlin somehow contrives in the twinkling of an eye.
That took the best part of a quarter of an hour of Pin and
patience to disentangle—especially patience, with the big fish
quietly head-and-tailing about every minute or so, just this side
of the round rock on the far bank. And that evening on the
way home, with seven sea-trout in the bag, I came over the hill
and there was the whole range of the West Highlands, from
Ben Nevis to Ben Cruachan, flushed an unbelievable rose pink
in the sunset.

That is the sort of memory which Pin could evoke. There
were many other tangles in which he was involved. There was
the classic tangle, the XXX of knots, made by two dachsie
puppies one evening under the willows of our little fishing
camp by the Lower Bringhi in Kashmir. There were tangles by
the Wiltshire Avon, below the bridge at Durrington, with the
"bump-bump" of the guns on the Westdown ranges and the
drone of an old Avro overhead as accompaniment. There was

a heart-rending tangle below a weir on the Bere stream, righted just in time to drop a little Olive Dun over a lovely 2-pounder feeding at the root of the run. I never caught another decent fish there.

This is all very well, but, after all, Pin was primarily designed to fix a hunting tie. It is difficult today to recapture that lift of the heart with which one stuck him through the stiff white folds on so many grey mornings in the past. I think it was my mother-in-law who first gave me the tip that, if one first stuck him through a bit of soap he would then slide smoothly through the starchiest folds of a tie without turning it into that passable imitation of a young cauliflower that used to burgeon below so many chins.

★   ★   ★

How many happy memories of fox-hunting could Pin bring back! The South Oxfordshire—my first love—Sam Ashton's voice hunting hounds, and the endless arguments about it all after dinner, while the level in the port decanter steadily dropped; Dick O'Connor and Stanley Clarke charging the Hazeley Brook; Anthony Muirhead, urbane and immaculate, a watchful eye on the day's events for his column in *Horse and Hound*; Bicester Thursdays, a fox away from Chearsley Firs, heading for Gipsy Bottom (how heavy that could ride in a wet winter); the first breath-taking experience of big Irish banks, in the Duhallow country, and the stone walls of Limerick; the Grafton, surely the biggest country in England, a nice hunt from Silverstone with Uncle Arthur flying the big fences as though he were 25 instead of nearly 70; glorious days from Cranwell— in the vale below Leadenham where the big ditches always seemed to be towards you or over the little stone walls on the Heath; a never-to-be-forgotten hunt from Croxton on a hireling, I think the slowest horse I ever rode (there are very few hunts you can't see on a slow horse if he can really jump, and if you watch hounds and use your head); the Peshawar Vale, a straight-necked Jack heading for Mohmand country, the brilliant green of young paddy against a backcloth of the Frontier hills under the egg-shell blue of early morning in Christmas week.

Is it a come-down from fox-hunting to a drag? I don't think so. A different sport, but what fun!—anyway, for those who were lucky enough to have good horses. What a zest it did add to life on those Tuesday and Friday mornings of the winter terms at Camberley, in the happy days before the horse disappeared from the British Army, when one stuck Pin through the tail of an ordinary tie—no question of a "stock" here. My father-in-law strongly and, I think, rightly disapproved of a hunting tie in rat-catcher. The Swallowfield line, the "Arm of the Sea" on the Combined Ops line, with the visitors from Greenwich and Andover gallantly charging the obstacles on borrowed horses; Jack Dill on a young chestnut horse riding that nice line from Foliejohn Park along the Drift road and left-handed past Hawthorn Hill, where one could gallop the fences as they came, without bothering about marking flags; the Easthampstead Brook, with the "ghouls" in an anxious knot by the gate, on the landing side, waiting for husbands and fathers to come down the hill and either sail proudly over the Brook or disappear ignominiously into its yawning depths. What fun it all was!

★   ★   ★

But what had Pin to do with jheels? Well, I have never been any good at wringing the neck of a wounded bird. The long steel shaft of Pin, thrust in at the base of the skull, brought a quick and clean and, I am sure, almost painless end. So he could evoke many memories of cool winter mornings in India; solitary snipe-shoots on Sunday morning from Delhi; a Christmas week-end in the Muttra Kadir with the A.O.C.; Noh jheel in the dawn with Dick Richardson, the Signals Wing Commander at Air Headquarters, bringing off shot after apparently impossible shot at high duck which I would never have dreamt of trying; driving black partridge out of patches of sugar-cane, a beater on either side of the patch with a cord between them, bowing and rustling the canes as they moved towards the guns,

"Time remembered is grief forgotten," and maybe those days in retrospect wear a rosier hue than they deserve. Maybe; but what fun we had!

And now, Pin has gone. Still—there are worse places to end one's days than in a quiet field among the friendly hills of Merioneth, with the salmon leaping in the pool below the road, the Welsh Black cows grazing overhead and the partridges calling in the stubble. And perhaps—who knows?—one day Tom or Evan or Emrys will have a tale to tell, of how they were ploughing the eleven-acre field and looked down and there, glinting in a furrow was a great old gold Pin.

12   Wilfrid Freeman and the Tools
of Victory, 1940

At this time, when we commemorate the great deliverance of
the Battle of Britain, our thoughts naturally turn to the words
of the Prime Minister's splendid contemporary tribute. For
most of us, the "few" to whom he voiced a nation's debt were
the pilots, those men whose "frozen trails looped white across
the blue" we watched with bated breath nearly thirty years
ago: their fame is secure indeed.

There were others, to whom it was not given to share
directly in that high adventure, but who surely have their place
among the few to whom the many owe so much. The delayed
action of long selfless years of strain and overwork still adds
names to the roll of those who died in battle. And high among
those names will stand that of Wilfrid Freeman. It was to him,
more than any other man, that the nation and the R.A.F. owed
the fact that the pilots of Fighter Command never ran short of
those aircraft whose names—"Hurricane" and "Spitfire"—are
now as much a part of British history as Nelson's *Victory* and
Royal Sovereign.

The fighter pilots obviously could not have done the job
if they had not been given the tools. I want here to discuss
this tremendous business of aircraft production, which was
Freeman's massive contribution to victory and is his prime
memorial.

The first step in the process is the job of the Air Staff, what
we call "operational requirements": what sort of aircraft we
want; what performance—that is, speed, range, ceiling and so
on; what armament we want—how many guns of what calibre,
or rockets, or, in these days, air-to-air guided missiles; what

loads of bombs and what sort; what radio and radar equipment
—all that sort of thing.

It is not easy. In these days, even before the last war, the
cycle of production—that is, the time it takes for an aircraft to
get from the drawing board into a squadron, so to speak—is
measured in nearly as many years as it took months with the
small, simple aeroplane of thirty years ago. That means the Air
Staff have to think a long way ahead, and not only use their
imagination and their knowledge of what a potential enemy is
up to, but also know what is technically practicable and how
long it is going to take to develop it. And then there is the awful
decision as to when to harden one's heart and go to production,
and wait no longer for the "something still better" that is
always just round the corner.

Before the war, that process and the subsequent business of
research, development, and production, were all the responsibility of the Air Ministry. In 1940 the Ministry of Aircraft Production came into being (as you probably know, since the war
it has been merged with the Ministry of Supply)[1] and they took
over responsibility for research and development and production. So, from then on, the Air Staff had to work in the closest
day-to-day co-operation with the M.A.P., as it was called. And
Britain was indeed fortunate in having, at a supreme crisis in
her history, Freeman, a man of genius who not only laid the
foundation of the production programme in the Air Ministry
before the changeover, but was later to steer it to its ultimate
development as Chief Executive in the M.A.P.

I believe I can best give you an idea of the problems of an air
production programme, and of the qualities required to solve
them, by telling you something about that man. I suppose no
other among the great men of the late war—and I choose that
description deliberately, well knowing that it is commonly
over-worked—was so little known to the public as Wilfrid
Freeman. He had a scornful horror of personal publicity. But,
though there have been other famous supply officers, and other

[1] It has now (1966) been merged in the Ministry of Technology.

regular soldiers who have gone on to achieve great reputations in business or industry, Freeman was pre-eminent among both. It was relatively late in life that he first embarked on the great industrial adventure which is a modern armament production programme. He was 48 when he came from being Commandant of the Staff College to the Air Council as Air Member for Research and Development at the outset of the Air Force expansion in 1936. And in June 1938 that appointment was extended to include production. So Freeman became the first man to be responsible for the whole process, from research to the production of the finished article.

He had been one of the pioneers of military aviation, and had made a great name for himself in the Kaiser's war. It was my good fortune to know him from early days, when he came out as a young Squadron-Commander to the Middle East in 1915; and even then there was no mistaking that he was something out of the ordinary. In later years, as Assistant Commandant at the Staff College, on the Air Staff under Trenchard, in command of the Central Flying School, or as Air Officer Commanding in Palestine, Wilfrid's personality and boundless energy were an inspiration and a challenge to all of us who worked with him or under him. He was as quick as lightning; the living antithesis of pomposity; a great lover of books and music, and a man of culture in the best sense of that often abused word. He was intensely human, critical but never unkind, with an impish, unpredictable humour and a capacity for selfless loyalty, that were at the same time the despair and delight of those to whom he gave his friendship.

The Battle of Britain fighters had been designed and brought to the verge of production before Freeman came into the Air Ministry. The decision to establish "shadow" factories, based on the motor-car industry, was also taken before his time. But the development and production of the Hurricanes and Spitfires were his responsibility; indeed, that is true of all new types from 1936 to the middle of 1940. He sponsored the great extensions of the "shadow" factories, and the creation of a vast reserve of manufacturing capacity, and vigorously nourished the design resources of what were known as the "family" firms. There were many decisions of vital importance during the years 1936 to 1939 for which the responsibility and the credit lay with Freeman. Hundred-octane fuel, the variable-pitch propeller, the air rocket, for instance; and, above all, the initiation of the four-engined bomber policy. I well remember, as Director of Plans, the excitement and interest of discussing with him his proposals for the first production orders of those aircraft, which were destined to have such a tremendous influence on the outcome of the war.

An essential quality in any man in his position is willingness to accept responsibility, to back his own judgment, and to run risks. That was a quality with which Freeman was supremely endowed. Some of his most important and fruitful decisions, such as to order the Mosquito or go ahead with Whittle's jet, were taken against formidable technical advice, and involved running real risks.

Between his appointment in 1936 and the time when in 1940 he became Vice-Chief of the Air Staff to Portal, the aircraft industry multiplied at least eightfold, and the monthly output of operational types had risen from a few score to about 800. Even more important, in that period there was a veritable revolution in technique, with the introduction of the all-metal, stressed-skin, high-speed monoplane. That was a reflection of another of Freeman's characteristics—his invariable insistence on quality, if necessary at the expense of quantity. Nowhere is that more important than in air warfare, but it took a man of Freeman's calibre to go on insisting on it, and get his way, in times when popular and political pressure was all for bigger and better numbers.

By 1940 there had been built up under the Air Ministry a working organization which made the transition to a separate Ministry a relatively easy matter. A man who was in a better position than most people to know—Lord Hives of Rolls-Royce—has written to me: "It was the expansion which was carried out under Wilfrid's direction in 1937–39 which enabled the Battle of Britain to be won. Without that foresight and imagination, no efforts in 1940 would have yielded any results."

From 1940 to 1942 Freeman was Vice-Chief of Air Staff and directed the internal policy governing the war-time expansion of the R.A.F., which was so ably carried into effect by his colleague, Air Marshal Courtney, the war-time Air Member for Supply and Organization. Lord Portal has said of him: "In this work, as in all he did, Wilfrid Freeman was a tower of strength. He was brilliantly successful in foreseeing the needs of the Service and in weighing the many conflicting factors and opposing views which had to be taken into account. He showed real genius for distinguishing what was right from what was merely clever, for finding the truth and exposing the superficial and the specious. And he displayed the most steadfast courage in making and defending many crucial and difficult decisions."

Two years later, at the insistence of the Prime Minister, he went back to the great task of production, as Chief Executive at the M.A.P. I think his experience as V.C.A.S. was useful to him there. He had seen how essential it was for the Air Staff to have a realistic forecast of production, on which to plan and organize the expansion of the Service, in place of the optimistic amateur estimates with which we had been familiar. His most conspicuous achievement in this second period was, of course, output—production almost doubled between 1942 and 1944. This meant piloting the industry through all the crises and shortages that are bound to arise in war time to the smooth and efficient peak of 1944.

It was not given to Freeman to stand in the limelight as the commander of great air forces in battle. But the task of providing the men with the tools calls for qualities no less great, and rarer. Freeman had the essential qualities of character, and the basic wisdom. He knew how to get on with other people, how to work a priority system with due regard to the needs of other branches of the war effort as well as his own. He had an unerring instinct for the real essentials; he knew that the best is the

5*

enemy of the good. And his understanding of technical problems—without being himself a technician—gained him the complete confidence of the industry. Above all, though obviously he could be known personally only to a few, his personality inspired real devotion right down the line: in the R.A.F., among Civil Servants, and in the industry.

Freeman would be the last man to claim all the credit. He was fortunate in serving under Ministers like Swinton and Stafford Cripps. He had some supremely able colleagues: men like Craven and Rowlands, Henry Self and Plowden, Lemon, Tizard and Sorley. And the industry itself threw up men of genius like Hives and Dobson, "A. R." Smith and Hennessy, the Nelson-Sheffield combination, and the de Havilland team. But I believe that no one who saw the Ministry of Aircraft Production at work in Freeman's time will be found to deny that virtually all the crucial decisions were taken, and all the risks faced, by Wilfrid Freeman.

So when, as each September comes round, we pay our tribute to the pilots of the Battle of Britain, and the airmen who kept their aircraft flying, let us remember also the men behind the front who gave them the tools of victory.

In the early morning of May 10 the Germans invaded Holland
and Belgium. By the afternoon of Sunday the 19th, ten days
after the initial attack, it became clear that the situation in
France and Belgium was becoming desperately dangerous, and
Gort for the first time had mentioned the possibility of a withdrawal towards the coast. The B.E.F. was falling back under
pressure towards the Scheldt. While the French Seventh Army,
from Walcheren and Beveland, and the Belgian Army on the
left of the B.E.F. were retreating, the French Armies on its right
were beginning to disintegrate—in fact Corap's Ninth Army,
upon which had fallen the main brunt of the break-through at
Sedan, had already disintegrated, and the First, on the immediate right of the B.E.F., was not far from collapse. In particular,
the onrush of the enemy armoured spearheads towards Péronne
and Cambrai presented a terrible threat and it was obvious that,
unless they could be checked, the B.E.F. would be cut off from
its bases and hemmed in in the Pas de Calais. The obvious thing
to do, if it was still possible, was to swing back the whole of the
left wing of the Allied Armies to somewhere like the line of the
Somme, there to form a fresh integrated front. But the possibility of any such thing was becoming increasingly doubtful,
as Gort evidently thought. It was therefore decided that the
C.I.G.S. should go over with instructions from the War
Cabinet, and the C.A.S. instructed me to accompany him to
concert with Charles Blount,[1] commanding the R.A.F. component with the B.E.F., any action that might be practicable
and necessary to conform with whatever arrangements might

[1] Air Vice-Marshal C. L. B. Blount, O.B.E., M.C., an old friend from whom
I had taken over 4 squadron at Farnborough fifteen years before. He was shortly
afterwards killed in a crash at Hendon.

be made to cope with an uncertain and increasingly dangerous situation.

We received our instructions at a meeting at 7.30 p.m. that Sunday evening in the Upper War Room at the Admiralty, under Mr. Churchill (by then Prime Minister), at which the three new Service Ministers and the Chiefs of Staff were the others present. The atmosphere in that long room was grave and tense, and during the discussion one's eyes could not but keep straying to the big map on the end wall with the strip of blue tape showing the terrible bulge spreading towards Arras and the coast. It was a pretty grim introduction to their responsibilities for the new Service Ministers, Mr. Eden, Sir Archibald Sinclair and Mr. A. V. Alexander. After some discussion, which had to be cut short because there was a special train waiting at Charing Cross to take us to a destroyer at Dover and there was some question of tides, the Prime Minister dictated the following order, which was taken down in longhand by Group-Captain Elliot[2] and Colonel Hollis of the War Cabinet Secretariat:

1. The Cabinet decided that the C.I.G.S. was to direct C.-in-C. B.E.F. to move southwards upon Amiens, attacking all enemy forces encountered and to take station on the left of the French Army.
2. C.I.G.S. will inform General Billotte[3] and the Belgian Command, making it clear to the Belgians that their best chance is to move south between the B.E.F. and the coast.

There was a short silence. Someone suggested that, as the B.E.F. was under the orders of General Georges, he should be consulted. A paragraph was added to the order to the effect that the War Office would inform him. The same thought was probably passing through other minds than mine—was the

[2] Now Air Chief Marshal Sir William Elliot, G.C.V.O., K.C.B., K.B.E., D.F.C. His last appointment in the Service was British representative on the Standing Group in Washington in the difficult years 1951 to 1954, where he established for himself a position comparable to that of Sir John Dill ten years earlier.

[3] General Billotte commanded Army Group No. 1, comprising a total of fifty-one French and British divisions.

War Cabinet in a position to direct operations of the B.E.F. from London, not really knowing the latest situation? What would be the reactions of the French Command, of whose forces it formed only a relatively small part? If the situation was really as black as it looked, was there in fact any prospect of this order being carried into effect? But it was already clear that Billotte was not exercising—even if he could—the co-ordinating function that was his. The Prime Minister, fresh from his visit to Paris, where he had received from Gamelin himself the shattering news that there was no strategic reserve in hand, was obviously in a better position to judge the situation than any-one else in the room. Anyway, there was no point in further discussion in London; the thing was to get over and see Gort and find out the situation on the spot; the Prime Minister wished us good luck as we left for Charing Cross and our special train—I, for one, feeling that we were likely to need it. There was no time to get the order typed before we left, and I put Bill Elliot's manuscript in my pocket and made two long-hand copies of it on our way to Dover.

It was a fine night, and as we left Dover Harbour we could see from the destroyer's bridge the flash of bursting bombs from Dunkirk, Calais and Boulogne on the horizon ahead. Half-way over, an aircraft flying low passed just ahead of us and dropped something into the sea; the theory was that it was a German aircraft and the object dropped was a magnetic mine, so we were exceedingly thankful that the ship had been degaussed—actually I doubt now whether it was anything of the kind. Arrived off Boulogne, we found bombing still in progress and waited outside for several hours till it was over. Ironside was very tired and had wisely turned in for a rest, while Simson (the captain of the destroyer, a splendid chap who was killed by a bomb when his ship was sunk shortly afterwards) and I sat in his cabin and drank whisky and soda. Shortly before dawn we went ashore to find Jacky Crawshay,[4] neat and cherubic, wait-ing for us with the G.H.Q. Rolls. The roads were reasonably

[4] The late Captain J. Crawshay, Lord Gort's A.D.C.

clear and it did not take us long to get through St. Omer and Armentières, to Gort's château near Wahignies not far from Carvin.

It was an unpretentious modern house with a very well-kept garden, a trim lawn and neat flower beds ablaze with tulips. After a wash and shave in Jacky's room I came down to find only one other yet up and about, Gort himself, pacing up and down in the early morning sunlight on the lawn. He was in his usual imperturbable form, but soon made it clear that he thought the British Army was in a desperately precarious position. We discussed the problem of evacuation, and he said he was thinking of using Ostend, Nieuport and Dunkirk. I had taken the precaution of bringing with me a little rough sketch map showing the arcs of the Hurricane and Spitfire from Kentish bases, and urged him to get as far west as he could—if possible back to Calais and Boulogne where we should be able to put pretty effective fighter cover over him; Ostend and Nieuport were too far east for us to be able to help him at all. He fully appreciated the point but doubted whether he would be able to get back that far. It was a gloomy conversation, in marked contrast to the peaceful setting of that pretty garden, with no sign or sound of war; and I was filled with admiration for Gort, whose demeanour gave no outward indication of what must have been his inmost knowledge that he was in the grimmest position of any British Commander in history; he might have been on one of those early morning rides on the Ridge at Delhi four years before. If ever there was a gallant British officer, he was one.

From the conversation at breakfast—Lindsell, Henry Pownall (Gort's C.G.S.), and Roger Keyes just in from Brussels—it was perfectly obvious that it was too late to carry out the movement suggested by the Prime Minister. After breakfast we repaired to the Advanced G.H.Q. office, where Ironside produced the order of the night before. It caused a mild sensation. Gort and Pownall pointed out with some emphasis that the British Army was now engaged with the enemy well forward into Belgium, where they had been marching and fighting without respite for eight or nine days; and asked how they were expected to conduct a prolonged rearguard action back from the Scheldt while executing a flank march across the front of a number of enemy panzer divisions who had broken clean through the French armies on their right—let alone attack all enemy forces encountered. They said there was no possibility of the Belgian Army being able to conform to any such movement—a fact that was already pretty clear from Roger Keyes's description of the state of affairs in Brussels.

During this conference Oliver Leese[5] came in, looking tired, but with his usual air of amused resignation, to report that the enemy were very close to Arras and long columns of tanks were converging on the town; 12th Lancers had been ordered south to reinforce the Guards battalion and a battery already in the town.[6]

However, while realizing that the order bore no relation to the situation as it existed, Gort arranged to send the only division he had available to move southwards with a scratch lot of infantry tanks. There was already a division of young soldiers, who had been sent out for labour purposes and had nothing but their rifles, occupying some sort of line somewhere south of Bapaume. The situation of the French Armies on the right was far from clear, but it seemed likely that they were in a pretty disorganized condition; the Ninth had apparently completely disintegrated and the First was believed to have its right flank somewhere north of Douai. General Billotte had visited G.H.Q. the night before in a state of the utmost depression and had told them that of his French divisions one was *tres solide*, some were *solide* and the rest were *ferme*—a categorization that

[5] Later Commander of the Eighth Army in Italy, then acting as D.C.G.S. at G.H.Q.

[6] I have not checked this with the Official History. This whole account of our visit to G.H.Q. is based on a note I made of it shortly after our return, and is intended to show how we saw the situation at the time. Details of troop movements and dispositions may be inaccurate in the light of what we now know from official records.

had not left our people much wiser or more assured of the real condition of our Allies.

Having delivered his message from the Prime Minister, the C.I.G.S. went off to find Billotte, whose headquarters were at Béthune. Blount had not yet arrived at G.H.Q., so it was arranged that I should stay behind to see him, following on later in the Rolls to pick up Ironside at Béthune—a rash arrangement as it turned out.

Fresh news from Arras disclosed what looked like (and indeed was) a hideous threat to the line of communication of the B.E.F. From a conversation with Lindsell it was clear that unless this drive by the enemy armour could be checked, the B.E.F. would soon be cut off from its ammunition and rations. Headquarters Air Component had been asked to do what they could to stop it, but they had no bomber force and we were out of touch with Barratt and his A.A.S.F. down in the Rheims area. At about 9 a.m. the threat looked so mortally dangerous that I made a signal to D.C.A.S., asking that, as well as the A.A.S.F., the Blenheims of 2 Group should be laid on under fighter cover from home bases, to attack tank spearheads and supporting columns converging on Arras. Actually, it was too late, and anyway air support laid on in this haphazard last-minute fashion cannot hope to be effective—as I should have known. But for the first time it had really dawned on one that there was every chance of the B.E.F. being rounded up and captured *en masse*, without a round of ammunition to enable them to continue fighting; and any steps seemed justified that held out the faintest hope of averting such a catastrophe.

Charles Blount turned up at about 10 a.m., looking utterly exhausted; he had had little sleep for a week and getting from his H.Q. through the stream of refugees that were by now blocking the roads was a terrific job. We made a hurried plan— I quote from the contemporary note:

His Blenheims had already gone to England that morning and their personnel was being got away through Calais and Boulogne, their transport going to Cherbourg. Three of his Army Co-operation squadrons had also already gone to the United Kingdom.[7]

5 Signals Wing, the Arras filter, R.D.F. stations and air stores parks had also cleared out to Cherbourg.

We arranged that 14 Group (fighters) should operate for the rest of the day from aerodromes in France, and the aircraft should then fly home that night. We decided that it was no good trying to move the fighters back to the Abbeville-Poix area, as we originally thought, and arranged that the transport and ground echelons should, if possible, go back to the Havre–Rouen–Beauvais–Paris area. I said we would operate 14 Group fighters from Kent aerodromes until we heard that the ground echelons had got through to Beauvais, and that in any event we would build up refuelling and servicing units as quickly as possible in the Beauvais area.

We recognized full well that the ground echelons might not get through in time to the Beauvais area, and I promised to get as much shipping as possible to Ostend, Dunkirk, Calais and Boulogne and to send as many transport aircraft as we could to get out the men.

It was obviously impossible to continue to operate squadrons in that part of France, and Lord Gort agreed that it was in the best interests of the B.E.F. as a whole to get squadrons either out to England or right back to the Seine as quickly as possible.

I then went off in the Rolls to pick up the C.I.G.S. at Billotte's H.Q., where I also hoped to get some roads allotted for the rearward movement of the R.A.F. transport columns. I hadn't gone far before it became clear that this latter was a vain hope. Five or six hours before, when we had arrived at Wahignies, the flood of refugees had not yet reached that place; by now, the state of the roads was indescribable, and I was lucky not to take more than the three hours it did take to do the eighteen odd miles to Béthune. Two streams of refugees were on the move more or less at right angles to each other—the flood from Arras moving north-west and that from Lille moving south-west; the resulting chaos had to be seen to be believed, and was accentuated by machine-gunning from the air.

[7] Arrangements had been made for a rear H.Q. to operate them from Kentish bases until fresh airfields could be made available for them back in France.

Every road and lane was chock-a-block with the pathetic flood —everything from motor cars and farm carts to wheelbarrows and perambulators, bicycles and little trollies drawn by dogs, piled with mattresses, cooking pots and odds and ends of household property, and everywhere the heartbreaking streams of wretched, frightened people mingled with exhausted stragglers from the Belgian and Dutch Armies, thick as a crowd coming away from a Cup Final.

When I reached the École des Filles at Béthune, which was Billotte's H.Q., the 12th Lancers were on their way through towards Arras, tired and dirty but in very good order under their colonel, Herbert Lumsden, whom I had last seen riding a winner at Sandown. The Army Group H.Q. was just packing up to move to Lillers and there was no sign of Ironside. That H.Q. made my blood run cold. It was like a morgue. I wandered down a long corridor on the first floor, looking into room after deserted, untidy room until I found one where there were a few utterly dejected-looking officers wandering listlessly about or sitting staring at the wall while an orderly rolled maps and packed up office gear. An English-speaking staff officer told me Ironside had gone back to G.H.Q. and wished me to join him there; when I tried to broach the subject of roads for our transport columns I drew (perhaps not unnaturally) a complete blank; but what gave me as far as I can remember my only actual experience of feeling the little hairs on the back of my neck standing on end were some words I distinguished in the *sotto voce*, half understood conversation—*"rien à faire"*, *"fini"*, and for the first time, that ghastly word "armistice".

I went out into the corridor and stood looking out of the high, dirty windows, watching clouds of smoke billowing upwards in the far distance into a cloudless sky, and a couple of Hurricanes shooting down a German aeroplane, and thinking —What hope for the B.E.F. if this is the staff of the Army Group supposed to be controlling their destinies?

A few minutes later, when I was trying vainly to get through to G.H.Q. on the telephone in the dusty entrance hall, the staff trooped down the stairs, and as they passed they all shook hands with me, their faces like death, and disappeared into the chaos outside to find their way to Lillers. Poor chaps, my heart bled for them—I expect many of them later fought gallantly with the Resistance or the Free French Army—but I have seldom been more frightened in my life.

The Rolls was outside in the street, and I was wondering how on earth I was ever going to get back through the refugees to G.H.Q., when Providence came to my aid in the form of an extremely smart sergeant of the Royal Military Police with a motor-bike. "Want to get to G.H.Q., sir?"—"Certainly, sir" —"Follow me if you please." How that marvellous man and the excellent driver of the G.H.Q. Rolls did it I shall never know, but they put their hands down on their horns and kept them there, and we went through those streams of refugees like a hot knife through butter—now in the road—now on one pavement and now on the other—cannoning off a farm cart full of children into an ancient Tilbury piled with bedding and suit-cases, dodging round trees and scattering the unhappy refugees left and right—we were back at G.H.Q. in almost a quarter of the time it had taken me to come. Ironside was there waiting, and after putting down a couple of large gins which Jacky Crawshay prescribed for my nerves after that drive, we set out again in the Rolls to get back to Calais, where arrangements had been made for the Flamingo with a Hurricane escort to pick us up that evening at St. Inglevert airfield.

We were out of luck. The arrangement was for the Flamingo to be at St. Inglevert at 6 p.m.; but we had left G.H.Q. far later than we had intended, the state of the roads was such that it took us nearly five hours to get back, and by the time we arrived at St. Inglevert there was no sign of the Flamingo or escort, but there was a stick of very fresh-looking bomb craters near the single hangar. Dowding had issued personal instruc-tions that they were not to wait there more than a certain time —he wasn't going to have a flight of his precious Hurricanes bombed on the ground if he could help it. There was nothing for it but to make our way into Calais in the hope of finding a bed. We went first to the harbour to see if by any chance there was a Naval craft which could take us over. But Calais harbour was not then a place one hung about in if it wasn't strictly necessary; the terminus station was deserted and all the windows broken, but as a forlorn hope I picked up a telephone in an empty office—and within two minutes was talking to my own office in the Air Ministry, and arranging for the Flamingo and escort to pick us up at 6 a.m. next morning!

Calais was full to overflowing and we were lucky to meet the Naval Transport Officer and the Military Landing Officer, who were looking forward to a night of getting troops and vehicles away as soon as darkness made it safer to bring shipping into the harbour, and who offered us their rooms in a little pub in a back street, where we were soon down to an excellent dinner and a bottle of Beaujolais that sticks in my memory.

Bombing started again as soon as it got dark, but we were too exhausted to bother about that and I was soon sound asleep between the M.L.O's sheets. I was awakened in the dim twilight of very early dawn by a babel of excited French voices in the narrow street outside my window. It was not yet time to get up and I lay with my eyes shut trying to remember the French for "Shut up!" I finally remembered the notices in French railway carriages in the Kaiser's war: "Taisez-vous—Méfiez-vous—les oreilles ennemis vous écoutent!" Getting out of bed to go to the window and shout "Taisez-vous", I was surprised to find the floor covered with broken glass; I was still more surprised on reaching the window to find that the house immediately opposite, which I had seen when I went to bed the night before, was no longer there, and in the midst of a gesticulating assembly of the local populace in the street below was the enormous figure of the C.I.G.S. fully dressed. I then realized that I was capable of sleeping, not only through one of the greatest earthquakes in history, but in between the last two of a stick of bombs, one of which demolished the café just behind the hotel and another a house within about thirty feet of my bed.

The operations of the special duty squadrons of the R.A.F. in the Mediterranean in 1944 were by no means confined to Yugoslavia. Throughout the year 624 Squadron, joined in the spring by an American unit under Major McCloskey, had been working from Blida in Algeria to the Maquis in the Massif Central,[1] with results that were to pay a valuable dividend when *Dragoon* was eventually launched in August. All Special Operations air activities in the theatre, other than those to the south of France, were co-ordinated by A.O.C. Balkan Air Force, and Elliot's squadrons of 334 Wing at Brindisi and Bari worked to the resistance groups in Northern Italy and ranged widely over Hungary, Rumania, Bulgaria and Greece. But the special operations which made the most exacting demands on the squadrons and were to be the subject of the greatest worry to me were those to Poland.

I always had a sense of special obligation to the Poles, though I cherished no illusions about them. Their dislike and distrust of the Russians were easily understandable even then—and were to prove more than justified by the tragic events of August and September 1944. But politically they could be very difficult and tactless, and sometimes tragically unwise—they were too often their own worst enemy and the despair of those who most wanted to help them. Nevertheless, I liked them and admired their courage. I could not forget the early weeks of the war, when we had been the helpless spectators of their country being

[1] My daughter Judy was by this time in the F.A.N.Y. employed by the Special Operations H.Q. near Algiers working to the Maquis. We used occasionally to take an afternoon off together, and go and bathe somewhere along the coast and forget the war. She visited me later in Caserta, have thumbed a quite unauthorized ride in the tail turret of a Liberator being delivered for 205 Group.

overrun and their Air Force being wiped out; I remembered particularly the feeling of impotence when, during a visit with Newall to Gamelin's headquarters at Vincennes in September 1939, I had watched the finger of Colonel Petibon, his Chief of Staff, tracing on the map the inexorable closing of the German grip on Warsaw. I had been present in Newall's office when the head of their Mission in London came to tell him that the Polish Air Force had ceased to exist as an entity, and to ask that Polish airmen who escaped might be accepted to carry on the fight in the R.A.F. During the Battle of Britain I had watched 303 Squadron pile up their magnificent record of achievement and sacrifice; and in the following year had stood on the terrace of my headquarters at Grantham in the gathering dark, and watched the Polish bombers from I Group on their way to Berlin and the Ruhr—their crews knowing full well that, if they fell into German hands, they would in all probability be butchered in cold blood. The Poles may have been tactless and often stupid, but they were indomitably brave.

So throughout that summer of 1944, as the Red Army drove the Germans back into Poland, I had always insisted on the Polish partisans getting all we could give them whenever the weather made it possible, often in the face of considerable pressure to use my special duty squadrons for urgent commitments elsewhere. I was still guileless enough to believe that the single-minded concern of our Russian Allies, like our own, was the defeat of the Germans, to which the effort of the Polish underground resistance groups could make a valuable contribution. Air supply to Poland was always the most difficult and dangerous of our special operations from the Mediterranean. The dropping-zones were anything between seven and nine hundred miles from base, mostly over enemy-held country, and there was little or nothing in the way of meteorological information or radio aids in the area. Our resources were pretty meagre—in fact the only units with the necessary range were 1586 (Polish) Flight and 148 Squadron R.A.F., which that summer averaged between them about a couple of dozen

Halifaxes. By the end of July there were not even that number available. Heavy casualties in the past two months had joined with technical troubles to reduce the numbers which we could put into the air on any given night; and actually the plan was to re-equip the squadrons during August and September with the Stirling, which was already being used in the special duty squadrons in England.

Then at 5 p.m. on August 1, the Polish Underground Army in Warsaw under General Bor came into the open and went into action against the Germans in the city.

What followed gave me I think about the worst six weeks in my experience. But it deserves description in some detail for much better reasons than that. It is a story of the utmost gallantry and self-sacrifice on the part of our air-crews, R.A.F., South African and above all Polish; of deathless heroism on the part of the Polish Underground Army fighting against desperate and increasingly hopeless odds in the tortured city of Warsaw; and of the blackest-hearted, coldest-blooded treachery on the part of the Russians. I am not a naturally vindictive man; but I hope there may be some very special hell reserved for the brutes in the Kremlin who betrayed Bor's army, and led to the fruitless sacrifice of some 200 airmen of 205 Group and 334 Wing. It is usually considered easy to be wise after the event, but Yalta and Potsdam were after the events of August and September 1944; and those of us who took part in those events may surely be excused if we fail to understand the attitude towards Stalin and the Russians exemplified in the later chapters of Robert Sherwood's book on Harry Hopkins. How, after the fall of Warsaw, any responsible statesman could trust any Russian Communist further than he could kick him, passes the comprehension of ordinary men.

To say this is not to suggest that the whole episode of General Bor's rising was handled wisely by the authorities of the Polish Government in London. Unhappily the very opposite is true. It was known, of course, that the Russians were approaching Warsaw, and their wireless had for weeks been broadcasting constant and specific appeals to the Polish partisans in Warsaw to rise and help the Red Army against the Germans. It was known that there was a substantial underground army in Warsaw under General Bor numbering some 43,000 in the city and a total of 175,000 in the Governorate-General of Warsaw. But there was no previous consultation or advanced planning either with the advancing Russians or with ourselves through S.O.E., on the nature of the action to be taken, or the support that could be afforded from outside. The Poles certainly had good reason for not consulting the Russians, who were already arresting those Polish partisan leaders who revealed themselves as the Red Army advanced—how good a reason was soon to be evident. But the failure of the exile Government in London and their Commander-in-Chief, the unhappy General Sosnkowski, to consult us in advance is difficult to excuse in the light of what followed.

The first intimation came on July 29—three days before the rising—in the shape of a letter from General Kukiel, the Minister of Defence, to General Ismay, followed on the 31st by a visit from General Tabor, the Director of Military Operations of the Polish Secret Army, to the head of S.O.E. They told us that arrangements had been made for the Underground Army to intervene in the imminent battle for Warsaw. Tabor said this might happen any time within the next four or five days—actually it happened the very next day—and presented a series of completely impossible demands from General Bor for various forms of air support. Unfortunately that gallant officer, as also Sosnkowski and Tabor, were land soldiers who had not the remotest conception of what was practicable as far as the air was concerned. Bor made four demands on us for assistance which he described as indispensable and which, for that reason, he should certainly have discussed with us before committing himself to action.

The first was for bombing of Cracow, Lodz and, as first priority, the environs of Warsaw. This could easily have been done by the Russians, but it was manifestly impossible for us to intervene with long-range bombers from England in a tactical battle in Poland. It would not have been a practical operation of war in any event, and the habitual refusal of the Russians to give us any information about their own positions or movements made it doubly impossible. Secondly, they asked for Polish fighter squadrons to land in the Warsaw area and take part in the battle, as a symbol of Polish efforts to free their country from the German invader. Any airman could have told them that this was fantastic. They seem throughout to have ignored the fact that Warsaw was separated from the nearest Allied air bases in the west by over 850 miles, and from those in Italy by more than 750 miles, almost entirely over enemy-held country; even if the squadrons had been able to land safely in the Warsaw area, they could not have been maintained in action. Their third demand was equally impracticable, largely for the same reason, and was that the Polish Parachute Brigade, then under the orders of S.H.A.E.F., should land in Warsaw. Their last was the only one that had a chance of being met, and even that not to anything like the extent they needed; they asked for substantially increased air supply, particularly of heavy machine-guns, anti-tank weapons, ammunition and grenades.

On August 2 the Polish Ambassador informed the Foreign Office that the rising had started the evening before. Early the next day I received a signal from the Chiefs of Staff to the effect that the Poles had appealed to the Prime Minister for supplies to be dropped into Warsaw that night, and that His Majesty's Government attached great importance to complying with this appeal if I thought it operationally practicable. I was told to report at once whether it could be done. The forecast weather that night was completely impossible and I said so at once, adding that it was not yet sure that the operation was practical at all for the special duty Halifaxes, and expressing the hope to Portal that he would not commit himself with the Poles until Elliot and I had had time to examine it further. I followed this up on the following day, August 4, with a signal (which had been agreed with Wilson) to say that I had reluctantly come to the conclusion that air supply to Warsaw was not a practical proposition, even if the weather was favourable; the aircraft would have to fly part of the way out and back in daylight and, with the moon at the full, would be bound to suffer some loss *en route*; to drop supplies accurately from a low altitude over a city which was bound to contain A.A. and machine-gun defences would mean that only a few would get through and much of the drop would fall into the wrong hands. In general, I said, we should achieve practically nothing and lose a high proportion of our heavy special duty aircraft. I pointed out that this project was the equivalent of the Russians attempting from Poland to support a resistance group in Florence, and urged that we should exert pressure on them to do the job themselves. This conclusion was reinforced that very night when five out of thirteen aircraft dispatched to various points between Cracow and Warsaw failed to return. As a result of this I told Portal that I did not intend to send more aircraft to any point in Poland in that phase of the moon.

I was never one to shrink from casualties if they were really justified. I hated them, as did all decent commanders; but it is sometimes necessary to face up to the fact that 500 casualties today may well save 5,000 in the next month. In this case, however, I was convinced that a prohibitive rate of loss to the Air Force could not conceivably affect the fate of the Polish Underground Army in Warsaw. It was one thing to drop supplies to pre-arranged dropping-zones marked by light signals in open country behind the lines, though even that was costing us dear in valuable lives. It was quite another thing to bring a big aircraft down to a thousand feet, flaps and wheels down to reduce speed, over a great city, itself the scene of a desperate battle and consequently a mass of fires and flashes from guns and bursting shells, and which I knew for certain (in spite of Sosnkowski's absurd assurances to the contrary) would be ringed by light A.A. weapons. I was convinced, and so it proved, that only a fraction of the supplies despatched would get into the right hands. I was not unconscious of the fact that commanders must sometimes accept casualties for what are narrowly called "polit-ical" reasons; and, as the battle dragged on, it was that alone which precluded me from refusing absolutely to send any more aircraft to Warsaw. But at the beginning it did not seem to me possible that the battle could last more than a few days—indeed, but for Russian treachery, it could hardly have done so; and I was unwilling to throw away valuable lives on such a forlorn hope, which could not possibly affect the issue of the war one way or another.

The Chiefs of Staff accepted my views and our Mission in Moscow was told to approach the Soviet General Staff. There then began a crescendo of political pressure by the Polish authorities in London of mounting and sometimes almost hysterical intensity. The Polish Prime Minister, Micolazyk, was away on his ill-fated visit to Moscow. But their President, Rakzkiewitz, bombarded Mr. Churchill; their Ambassador, Count Razcynski, the Foreign Office; and General Sosnkowski, the Chiefs of Staff and the Air Ministry, with piteous appeals and sometimes almost peremptory demands for the impossible. Their attitude is understandable in the light of the dreadful circumstances of the time. Poor Bor's position was desperate— his rising had probably been somewhat premature anyway, and he was insistently appealing for help. The exiled Government had to consider also the morale of the Polish people as a whole and of their forces fighting with us in the West, and they must not be blamed for exerting themselves to the utmost to help their men in Warsaw. The fault lay with Sosnkowski in initiating, or authorizing, without any previous consultation or planning, an operation which could only succeed if it received the outside support which the most elementary consideration would have revealed as impracticable. Even he perhaps may be forgiven for failing to foresee the depths to which Russian Communist treachery would descend.

It was, no doubt, inevitable that I should find myself under pressure. Portal and the Chiefs of Staff screened me as much as possible; they knew as well as I did that nothing I could do would have any real practical value, but they could not blind themselves to the political importance of at least making some gestures to help. The Polish Government also had their direct contacts in Bari in the Polish country section of S.O.E., who on one occasion even went so far as to issue an order direct to Squadron-Leader Krol of 1586 Flight to carry out an operation to Warsaw that I had forbidden, an "order" which, needless to say, I countermanded as soon as it was given. As early as August 5 Portal told me that the Poles had protested violently against my decision, and he said that, while there was no question of pressing me to do something that I considered certain to be costly as well as useless, even a token gesture might have far-reaching results on further relations between the Poles and the British.

For two days I stuck to my guns and refused to play. Then on the 7th I made a decision, very reluctantly, which has always rather weighed on my conscience, but was I think inevitable. Polish political pressure had become more and more violent, and the indomitable Krol and his crews were themselves pressing to be allowed to help their friends in Warsaw. I could readily understand the psychological reasons for doing something to sustain the morale of Bor's men and, having made my views unmistakably clear to the Polish Government, felt that as they insisted on risking the lives of their own crews on what I had told them was a forlorn hope, I could no longer stand in their way. I was not prepared to use British crews—at least until the last quarter of the moon. I therefore authorized a small effort from 1586 Flight, and on the nights of August 8th and 9th three and four Polish crews respectively were despatched to Warsaw. The fact that all seven aircraft had the luck to get away with it and that some of their containers reached the right hands was really a misfortune. It aroused false hopes in Warsaw and led to an intensification of political pressure in London with the result that, against my better judgment, I felt bound to send British crews as well as Poles to Warsaw when the moon entered its last quarter. On the 13th, with Wilson's agreement, I diverted from operations in support of *Dragoon* two of my four heavy squadrons of 205 (Bomber) Group, Nos. 178 R.A.F. and 31 S.A.A.F. By this time the Prime Minister had arrived in Italy and I discussed the affair with him, emphasizing my view that, if the Russians would not supply Warsaw, the only way of getting arms on any adequate scale to Bor was for the Eighth U.S. Bomber Command to do it from England, going on to land at Russian bases, for which they had made the necessary "shuttle" arrangements in connexion with the *Pointblank* offensive.

The weather was unfit on the 10th and 11th, but on the five nights between the 12th and 17th, though there was little or no moon, seventeen out of ninety-three aircraft despatched failed to return, three others crashed on landing owing to flak damage and many others were damaged and some of their crews wounded. The South African Liberator Squadron, No. 31, was particularly unfortunate, losing eight aircraft in four nights. Some supplies did get through to the Underground Army, but far more went adrift—some of the sorties were directed not to the city itself but to a dropping-zone in Kampinos Forest, of which the value to the Poles could only be described as slightly better than nothing. It could not go on. On the 17th I told Mr. Churchill that in my view, unless supplies could be sent in from England or by the Russians, Bor's army was beyond our help, and instructed Elliot to stop operations to Warsaw, though I was prepared to authorize sorties to other dropping-zones elsewhere in Poland. The egregious Sosnkowski immediately returned to the charge, insisting that Polish crews of 1586 Flight should continue to go, and demanding the transfer of some crews from 300 (Polish) Squadron in Bomber Command to make up their losses. By this time Portal also was in Italy visiting units, and Sir Archibald Sinclair, the Secretary of State, signalled him to the effect that, if I was still unwilling to send Polish crews to Warsaw, which he himself felt we should not refuse to do, the matter should be referred to the Prime Minister for decision. There were very few crews left in 1586 Flight, and Harris was understandably protesting against releasing experienced bomber crews for what he regarded as a useless political gesture. I had never yet been told what was the absolute minimum delivery essential to sustain Polish resistance in Warsaw but on the 20th elicited the information that it was ninety containers, or fifteen Halifax loads, per night safely delivered to the Poles, which was demonstrably far beyond anything we had a hope of doing. Nevertheless, after consultation with the C.A.S. in Naples, I very reluctantly agreed to allow Polish volunteer crews to continue, and for the next few nights when there was little or no moon, a trickle of supplies did reach Warsaw, fortunately without loss.

Then on the two nights of the 26th and 27th when the moon was in its first quarter, four aircraft out of nine despatched failed to return and another crash-landed at base with very severe flak damage, including two engines out of action; only one aircraft claimed to have reached the city. Elliot felt he could no longer allow even the gallant Polish volunteers to continue at this rate, and I again cancelled operations to Warsaw, telling Portal (who had by then returned to England with the Prime Minister) that I was completely convinced that it was useless to continue this effort, which by then had cost us twenty-five crews and achieved practically nothing. The C.A.S. backed me up, pointing out amongst other things that to continue to allow the Polish volunteers to go was putting the R.A.F. and our British crews in an increasingly invidious position. Unfortunately, the political factor was again too strong for us. I do not presume to criticize our Government for this—they alone could judge the broad political and strategic situation of which I, as the Commander-in-Chief on the spot, could only see one facet. Anyway, it was decided that, while I should not be precluded from cancelling operations which I felt had no chance of success, there should be no overriding decision to discontinue all operations to Warsaw from Italy.

So the grim story went on. On August 31 Portal informed me of the political decision that I should permit Polish volunteers to continue to go to Warsaw whenever I thought they had a chance of success, and asked me to consider using my British heavy squadrons dropping from above light flak range with the delay-drop supply parachutes, of which some had become available. In reply, while repeating my view that this was not a reasonable operation of war in relation to the practical results to be achieved, I told the C.A.S. that seven aircraft were laid on for less distant dropping zones elsewhere in Poland that night (September 1) and I would decide in the light of what happened to them whether, on subsequent nights, to allow Polish volunteers to resume dropping to Warsaw from a height above light flak range. Of these seven aircraft, four failed to return and only two claimed to have reached their dropping-zones, as a result of which I cancelled all operations till the last quarter of the moon. Actually there was only one more expedition from Italy to Warsaw in spite of continued political pressure. On the night of September 20, out of twenty aircraft, even using the high dropping technique, five failed to return. After that, fortunately, bad weather came to reinforce my continued protests. At the same time, the Russians having at last been shamed into allowing a shuttle operation, plans were made for a large-scale high drop by escorted bombers of the U.S. Eighth Air Force from England.[2] But at the beginning of October the inevitable end came and Warsaw capitulated. Bor's battle was one of the most gallant and desperate episodes in the whole bloody history of war, but the issue was never really in doubt. The only marvel is that he managed to hold out as long as he did.

Meanwhile, what of our Russian allies? Why, with the Red Army in the Warsaw suburbs, was it necessary that their Polish allies, fighting with small-arms in the city centre against German armour, should be supplied by British and Polish aircraft from bases on the Adriatic Coast, nearly 800 miles away? As I pointed out in one of my many signals, this amounted to sending aircraft from Iceland to drop supplies in Mayfair, though

[2] One large-scale drop by a hundred and four heavies of the U.S. Eighth Air Force was undertaken on September 18.

the Russians had their forward troops in Southwark, with air-fields in Middlesex. In operations on twenty-two nights during the two months of Warsaw's agony, that had cost us thirty-one heavy aircraft missing out of 181 despatched—a loss rate overall of more than seventeen per cent.

Immediately after the rising had begun, both we and the Poles had appealed to the Russians for help, and we had told them that we could not effectively supply Bor's army from our distant bases. On August 9th Mikolazyk told us from Moscow that Stalin himself had promised to supply all help to Warsaw and particularly to drop arms into the city. Nothing happened, and as early as the 15th I was telling Portal that it was difficult to resist the conviction that the Russian failure to supply War-saw was deliberate, though we in Italy were giving them all possible support in their own purely political (and incidentally perfectly safe) operations into Yugoslavia. On the 18th I sent a long signal to our Ambassador in Moscow asking him to let the Russians know that already since the beginning of August we had lost in operations to Poland twenty-one aircraft missing, three destroyed on landing and fifteen damaged by flak, includ-ing crews wounded. I said we were gladly giving all the help in our power to the Russian airmen at Bari, and I felt entitled to ask the Russian Air Force to help us out in Poland and save us having to continue these long-range operations at such terrible cost. I might have saved my breath had I seen an article in *Izvestiya* on the previous day, or Vishinsky's communication on the night of the 16th to the U.S. Ambassador in Moscow, which amply confirmed the suspicion I had voiced to Portal. Indeed on the 22nd Molotov came into the open and told our Ambassador flatly that the Soviet Government objected to British or American aircraft landing in Soviet-held territory while employed on dropping arms to Warsaw. This meant not only that American "shuttle" operations to their base at Poltava were barred but that Elliot's aircraft, even when damaged and with wounded men on board, had to face the long grind back through the enemy defences to their bases in Italy.

It was for obvious reasons impossible at the time publicly to voice the opprobrium which all decent men felt at this behaviour; but the British and American Governments expressed themselves in the strongest possible terms to the Kremlin, who apparently came to the conclusion that ultimately the effect to their treachery on world opinion might be more harmful of them than the survivors of Bor's army could ever be. Or maybe they felt that their ends had already been adequately achieved. Anyway, six weeks after the Warsaw rising Molotov climbed down and handed a note to our Ambassador to the effect that, if we were so firmly convinced of the value of supply to Warsaw and still insisted on Russian participation, the Soviet Government was prepared to agree. This shockingly belated reversal of form was tucked away in a preposterous homily. There was the old complaint that the Soviet High Command had not been consulted in advance—as though any normal human being would punish a military mistake by an ally by leaving him to be butchered by the enemy! We were told that had they been warned of the rising they would have advised against it, because by the time the Red Army reached Warsaw it was too tired to take the place by storm. Yet in the next breath they said that had they been warned in time, events in Warsaw would have taken a very different turn. Altogether it was a nauseating document. The plain fact is, of course, that the Kremlin never intended the rising to succeed. Their intention then in regard to Poland, was that which they have since put into effect—to make of it a vassal satellite state, and they had their Lublin Communist stooges all ready to take over. Nothing could have been more convenient for them than this opportunity to arrange for the Germans to do their dirty work for them and liquidate the Polish patriots who might have thwarted their intentions.

Before turning to subjects which leave a less nasty taste in the mouth, it may be worth mentioning one other example of Russian behaviour about a couple of months later, when we were still trying to supply Polish resistance groups engaged in

6

fighting the Germans. For some weeks I had been pressing through our Mission in Moscow for permission to fly over Russian-occupied territory on the way to the dropping-zone, so as to avoid having to run the whole gamut of German night fighter and flak defences. When at last the Soviet General Staff deigned to reply they refused, on the grounds that the bulk of our supplies dropped into the wrong hands, and anyway the only partisans they recognized were those known to and supplied by the Soviet forces—in other words the Polish quislings, who were helping the Russians to suppress their own people. As a matter of fact my reaction to this was to route our aircraft over Russian territory, in spite of an extraordinary protest from our Mission in Bulgaria that to do so would be provocative to the Russians; what they thought it would provoke them to do is not clear, except shoot us down, which I have no doubt they would not have hesitated to do if they could. Actually, there was no Russian reaction—probably because their air defence system was so inefficient that they did not know we were flying over them, which was what I counted on.

15   Epilogue: A Look at the Future, 1967

Happiness Is Freedom, and Freedom Is Courage[1]

We old men who are lucky enough to be able to look back and revive the memories of sixty years of crowded life have seen the passing of an epoch. That is a trite phrase, but true. No doubt old men a hundred years ago who had seen the beginning of the age of steam were saying the same—but with nothing approaching the same justification. Never before in history have men seen in their own lifetimes such stupendous changes in almost everything that touches human life and experience; whether for the better or for the worse is a matter of opinion, and anyway irrelevant. Actually, if we could be wafted by some magician's wand back a hundred years or two into what are loosely called the "Good Old Days", I doubt whether we should really find them as good as all that—except for a very few of the most fortunate. However that may be, life has changed in a manner and to a degree undreamt of even half a century ago, and we have to make the best of it. And the key to our ability to do that surely lies in the words of Pericles at the head of this chapter.

The Army in which I first went to war not much more than fifty years ago was basically the same sort of Army as those which fought under Marlborough at Blenheim and Wellington at Waterloo: Horse, Foot and Guns. True, it did include a few of those new-fangled flying machines, primitive stick-and-string contraptions, themselves considered marvels in their day. But the greatest volume of bulk tonnage that crossed the Channel in the Kaiser's War was forage for the horses, and Cavalry still fought with sabres and lances. Before I laid up my

[1] Pericles (a favourite quotation of Field-Marshal Smuts).

last uniforms in moth-balls, I had served through another Great War in which the horse—fortunately for him but, as I think, unhappily for man—was virtually unknown: a war in which the "Nations' Airy Navies" of Tennyson's dream rained thousands of tons of explosive upon the civilian populations of Europe, and ultimately obliterated two whole cities of Japan each with one deadly canister. I had been lucky enough to become the professional head of a Royal Air Force, just being equipped with great aircraft capable of carrying megatons of nuclear destruction at a speed of 500 knots and a height of 11 miles above the earth—themselves now obsolescent.

Today we have seen man-made instruments planted on the surface of the moon, and men walking in space while whizzing round the earth 200 miles high and at 18,000 miles an hour; yet we have not conquered the worst afflictions of man's mind and body. True, we have discovered how to prolong the span of men's lives—how to prevent them dying; we have yet to match that with the ability to prevent them being born in unwanted millions. Satellites, nuclear energy, television, computers, radar, jet aircraft spanning the Atlantic in a few hours with huge loads of passengers and freight—these and other marvels are commonplaces of our day. If I, as a young officer, had told my father that I should live to see these things he would have been acutely concerned, would have concluded (with every justification) that I was either drunk or crazy or both.

Perhaps a moral is that it is unwise indeed to assert that anything is impossible. One smiles tolerantly at people who enthuse about "Unidentified Flying Objects"; but who are we to say that they cannot be space-ships bearing human creatures from some planet in a state of scientific development thousands of years ahead of our own: another world in some vast galaxy so remote as to be beyond the comprehension of ordinary men?

*   *   *

I am not going to begin at my time of life to inflict upon long-suffering readers my views about Flying Saucers—as a matter of fact I have none, except that it is silly to say they are impossible. Like Gilbert's Noble Statesmen, I do not itch to interfere in matters which I do not understand. There can never have been an Air Force Officer less technically-minded; I have tried to hoist in just enough to free me from total dependence on the advice of experts—those people who know more and more about less and less—and to enable me to make a reasonable guess as to whether or not they are pulling a fast one on me; but if anyone tries to explain to me the detail of any technical gadgetry, I fall back on looking wise and saying "Quite"—a word which covers a multitude of sins and sometimes an ocean of ignorance.

In this book I have been looking back, trying to paint word-pictures of a now bygone age, in the hope that they may be of some passing interest and perhaps amusement to our grandsons and their generation. In this last chapter I shall try, perhaps rashly, to look ahead, setting down some random reflections on the kind of life to which they may look forward. So I hope I have made it clear that, in doing so, I shall certainly disappoint anyone who hopes to hear about the scientific wonders of the future: I am not foolish enough to peer into that particular crystal ball.

*　　*　　*

Let me start near home. We have for generations past been a supremely fortunate people in many diverse ways here in this island; and I take comfort from the belief that the younger generations can continue to enjoy many of the things which I think are of real importance to the good life—things which have made my own life well worth living—if only they will take the trouble consciously to preserve and cherish them. England is not all overspill and traffic jams and huge excrescences of glass and steel, like nightmare match-boxes standing on end. There are still things more truly characteristic of the British way of life than crime-waves and drug-addicts, bingo and bunny-clubs, lightning strikes and sex-orgies, pop-music and caravan parks. Beatniks and vandals, in true perspective, are no more than a nasty little fungus amid the healthy harvest of British youth. We old people tend to shudder at flowing locks and bizarre garments; but I don't think they look more silly to us than the "Oxford bags" and other embellishments of our youth—and I mean both sexes—would look to us today.

We have at the top the admirable example of a Royal Family who (despite the too frequent scurrilous outbursts of bad manners from insignificant quarters) are far more deeply rooted in the affection and respect of the people than were their forebears in my grandfather's day and earlier: an intelligent and beautiful young Queen with a consort who is an exemplar of what all young men should wish to be—as a man. That is a moral, a social and political asset beyond price, and it is our self-interest as well as our duty jealously to guard it. The discipline and fighting efficiency of the Queen's armed forces (or what is left of them) stand as high as ever they did. The Services are different from what they were in my day—not so much fun perhaps, more earnest and demanding on duty, more free and easy off it and (unfortunately) much more heavily married. But as a way of life there is nothing more worth-while. The Foot Guards troop their Colour today with meticulous smartness as they did in old King Edward's time; the Red Arrows change formation at the top of a roll with marvellous grace and precision; and the Royal Navy, though lamentably small, still maintains its great traditions of practical efficiency and devotion to duty.

By the way, I wonder if others have found, as I do, that one gets just the same *sort* of kick out of seeing anything supremely well done by the real top-class performer—no matter how different, and whether or not one understands anything of the finer points of the art: Margot Fonteyn dancing, Royal Marines doing arm-drill without orders, Oleg and Ludmilla Protopopov figure-skating, a Central Flying School team doing formation aerobatics, Lester Pigott or Pat Taaffe riding a winner—they all give me the same warm feeling of thrilled satisfaction.

We can still take refuge from the strain of life in cities and the feverish rush of motor-ways in a countryside whose beauty is unexcelled anywhere in the world: the soft flush suffusing April woods, splashed here and there with green of young beech and chestnut; the old gold of early oaks, bare elms with their busy clamour of high-nesting rooks, and a drift of blue-bells in a clearing like a patch of summer sky; distant hills raising a misty blue background to a pattern of spinneys and fields—chocolate of plough-land and the rich green of leys neat-striped by the harrow; the gentle glory of primroses on the banks of cuttings as the train flashes by—where else but England? Anyone who flies over it knows how largely it is still unspoilt. It can remain so: we *can* protect it from the depreda-tions of the jerry-builder; as also we can defend our field sports against the well-meaning busybodies who seem so curiously anxious to abolish sports which give pleasure and healthy exer-cise to others, while remaining consistently blind to the real cruelties like motorized deer-poaching in the Highlands.

Our farmers are as good as any in the world—better than most; our sleek cattle and blood horses still go overseas to enrich the stocks of many lands. Far from the roar of traffic and the reek of diesel fumes, the lithe red fox still steals the chickens and quickens the blood of man—still from "clubbed woods of winters day"[2] the lilt of a distant horn and the cry of hounds comes faint down the wind across leagues of English grass—despite the curse of wire.

> The autumn road, the mellow wind
> That soothes the darkening shires,
> And laughter, and inn fires.
> White mist about the black hedgerows
> The slumbering midland plain,
> The silence where the clover grows
> And the dead leaves in the lane,
> Certainly, these remain.[3]

★   ★   ★

[2] *The Land* by Vita Sackville-West.
[3] *The Chilterns* by Rupert Brooke.

From his rock amid the heather the old cock grouse still tells us to "Go back—go back"; pheasant and partridge still swing over the guns, and the flighting duck drops down to the moorland pool at dusk. The salmon still runs up from the sea to spawn, and in Hampshire chalkstreams and the tumbling rivers of Argyll the game trout still takes the angler's fly. These too remain and will gladden the hearts of men as they have in years gone by.

In spite of the disappearance of the horse from the Army, we have amateur riders over fences as good and gallant as ever in the past. On our T.V. screens today we can watch great horses —like the superb Arkle going out on to the course at Cheltenham or Newbury with that noble, swinging stride, and back to the winner's enclosure still on his toes with ears cocked, obviously enjoying every moment of it: the greatest 'chaser of all time, despite those of us who swore we should never see again the like of Golden Miller. At Twickenham and Murrayfield and Cardiff Arms Park we can still see glorious Rugger: we must be vigilant to preserve the standards of clean play that have always distinguished that great game; but in our Schools the promise for the future is as bright as ever. At Wimbledon, worthy successors to Fred Perry and Helen Wills still draw the summer crowds; and at Lord's and Old Trafford small boys still scramble for the balls over the boundary and besiege their heroes for autographs as they come off the field when stumps are drawn.

We can still enjoy beautiful pictures in our art galleries and (thanks largely to the National Trust) in many of our great houses, see the plays of Shakespeare and the light operas of Gilbert and Sullivan. The wireless has brought good music to millions who could never have heard it in the days of my youth. And on the last night of the Proms "Rule Britannia" and "Land of Hope and Glory" still lift the roof of the Albert Hall.

All these are part of the English heritage and will remain so for generations yet unborn—*provided* only that we really take the trouble to see that they do; and that involves, first and foremost, making sure that we can continue to afford them, by doing an honest job of work and not taking more out of the kitty than we put into it.

*   *   *

But Britain can never be an Island complete unto herself—what of the wider world beyond the seas that can never again be our sure shield?

For us, of course, the first cardinal condition is the close of the chapter of Empire. When I was a schoolboy our country was the richest and most powerful on earth. As a young officer—and for that matter as a not so young one—I saw the Union Jack flying and British uniforms on the dockside wherever the troopship touched, from Southampton to Ceylon and Singapore. This small island was the centre of the greatest Empire the world has ever seen; and in the two Great Wars of my time fighting men of the Empire from all over the world rallied to the support of the Mother Country. In less than a generation all that has passed into history, and today Britain ranks in the second category of power and influence. We have much more to be proud than to be ashamed of in our Imperial record, and our former subject peoples far more cause for gratitude than for resentment. We have sometimes been wicked and often silly—who has not? The Opium war of 1839 and our subsequent high-handed treatment of China are cases in point. And lesser lunacies like denying membership of clubs in India to educated Indians—even to officers holding the King Emperor's commission—aroused justifiable resentment. But by and large our rule was beneficent and unselfish. The Nabobs who made fortunes out of India in the old days were an insignificant minority compared to the administrators—the soldiers and men of the Indian Civil Service—who spent their lifetime (too often cut lamentably short by disease) in selfless service with miserably small reward except the satisfaction of a job well done. I would advise any young people who doubt that to read Philip Woodruff's *The Men Who Ruled India.*[4] But all that is over. And I think on

---

[4] Published by Jonathan Cape.

6*

the whole we of the older generation have not been too bad at the difficult job of mental adjustment to our new status in the world. I am sure Britain can and must (and in fact still does) continue to exercise an important influence in Asia and Africa, but of a different kind—mainly in the technical and economic, social and educational fields. I used to hope that the free multi-racial Commonwealth that followed Empire would be able to exert an influence even stronger, because more broadly based and more generally acceptable; but I am afraid it is only realistic to admit that in the sphere of international politics it has ceased to mean much—and in the strategic field means even less. Nevertheless (and here is a thought for the young) the cultural and social and racial links remain immensely valuable and full of hope. I think it difficult to exaggerate the importance to inter-national understanding and inter-racial tolerance of conscious effort and sacrifice to counter the centrifugal force of new-found nationalism, by sustaining and strengthening this residual legacy of Commonwealth. Incidentally, this is a field in which ideals go hand-in-hand with enlightened self-interest for a people who live by international trade.

Younger people are probably less resentful than their elders tend to be of what may sometimes seem precocious impudence on the part of some new Nations. And the young are right: these manifestations are symptoms of a phase that will pass and, however silly and unreasonable, are humanly understandable— I daresay we should have behaved much the same in their place. Do not let us get too impatient of all this nonsense about "neo-colonialism". I confess I am sometimes irritated by the habit of some of our new partners—when we do something that does not happen to suit them—of threatening to leave the Common-wealth, as though they were doing us a favour by staying in it; but this again should not be taken too seriously; if they want to leave the Commonwealth, let them get on with it and leave —it is not we who would be the losers. Too often they indulge in the luxury of abusing us and opposing us in the United Nations and elsewhere, without abating their insistent demands for economic aid. But we have got to try to understand these peoples' point of view and stop deluding ourselves that the British system of democracy, evolved over the centuries, is necessarily either suitable or practical in these new Nations, most of them generations behind us in so-called civilization and too often riddled with tribalism. Anyway we can take some comfort from the fact that the transition to independence of our former Imperial territories has—in spite of some black spots— been less chaotic and bloodstained than those of other former Colonial Empires. One serious weakness today is the loss of the intimate knowledge and sympathy on the part of British people who formerly lived and worked for years in Asian and African countries—in the old Indian Civil Service, the Colonial Services and the Army. Here is a great opportunity for the young to repair that loss by getting out into the world, mixing and working with people of different colours and creeds—if only for a year or two after leaving school, with pioneer ventures like V.S.O.[5] and Comex.[6] They could make no more valuable contribution to the greater understanding between Nations and races that is so desperately needed in this last third of the Twentieth Century.

So it is useless to bemoan the passing of Empire; I doubt whether in the long run we shall be worse off economically and —the world being what it is today—probably not politically: the old picture of a great maritime Empire—all that pink on the maps—is hopelessly out of date in a world that has been shrunk by Science to the proportions of an Hellenic City State. Today we are faced with a new kind of challenge—a new industrial revolution based on science and technology. We are admirably equipped to meet that challenge; but we can not do it alone. We must take our due leading place in a great European partnership, as a first stage in the evolution of a wider community. I shall have a bit more to say about that later on.

*   *   *

[5] Voluntary Service Overseas.
[6] The Commonwealth Expedition.

Meanwhile the world scene today is more chaotic and its future development less predictable than ever in my lifetime—or, I think, in history. It is no good bemoaning the fact that British Imperial power is no longer the massive instrument of world order and stability that it used to be—that the Royal Navy can never again enforce a Pax Britannica. I wonder whether anyone, anywhere in the world, is the happier for that—or indeed for the fall of the French and Dutch Empires—except the Boys who have got the Jobs. But there it is. We must recognize that we are in the throes of the greatest secular revolution in history. It is perhaps surprising that it should have taken as long as it has to reach its present peak after the Russo-Japanese war of 1904, which was the beginning of the end of the myth (the short-lived myth as history is measured) of White Supremacy. Anyway it was inevitable. And it surely gains its greatest impetus from the amazing growth in recent years of the media of mass communication, particularly the radio—pouring as it does—subversive poison into the ears of immature youth and of illiterate, under-privileged millions in squalid mud villages all over the world.

So much of the almost daily fare served up by Press and Radio nowadays is gloomy and depressing: the dreary, deadly squabble between India and Pakistan about Kashmir; the beautiful islands of Indonesia plunged by a dissolute maniac into economic ruin and internal strife; in the Middle East, the crows of Suez come home to roost—the apparently incurable enmity of the Arabs towards Israel fanned by Nasser's insatiable ambition and culminating in the fantastic six-day war of June 1967 —of which we have yet to see the real end; the endemic instability and lack of unity in the so-called Arab Nations, Egypt and the medley of dusty little States between Turkey and the Indian Ocean; the terrible outbursts of racial hatred and violence in the United States—which we may see reproduced in our own country if we are not careful; ceaseless wars and revolutions in what was French Indo-China—in particular, of course, the brutal war in Vietnam, for which it is all too easy for people with no responsibility to abuse the Americans.

In Africa, how lamentable that so many new Commonwealth Nations, to say nothing of the Congo, should be so busy proving how right were those who warned against supercharging the Wind of Change by rushing the grant of independence so prematurely. But it was probably inevitable; the fact surely is that the British public, rightly or wrongly, are not willing to continue to pay in lives or money for more Mau-Mau rebellions or Malayan "emergencies". South of the Zambesi—what a tragic disappointment it was that we should have been so near agreement, only to have our hopes dashed by the cardboard Canutes of the Rhodesian Front. My head tells me that the policy of successive British Governments there has been broadly right—and anyway inevitable in this day and age; my heart has always rebelled at the thought of Rhodesians and South Africans being so bitterly estranged from us: the soldiers who fought with us at Delville Wood and in the Desert, the air crews who served under me in Italy and shared with their British and Polish comrades the glory of that desperate forlorn hope over Warsaw. We have now no practical alternative but to go through with it, and must pray that the worst does not befall. It is impossible now to see through the murk ahead—the only thing that seems certain is that no one will be the better off, least of all perhaps the White Rhodesians. While always welcoming help and constructive advice from any quarter, we must not be deflected from our purpose by shrill reprobation on the part of critics (of any colour or political creed) who lack any responsibility or qualification to handle objectively a problem that calls for steady nerves and cool statesmanship.

Away in the Far East behind the bamboo curtain looms the enigma of Communist China, that gigantic country which was the home of an ancient and graceful civilization when we in this island were still blue-painted aborigines, now racked by an orgy of murder and hooliganism, intrigue and betrayal masquerading under the guise of "Cultural Revolution", and with its formidable millions of military man-power soon to be reinforced by nuclear weaponry. It would be foolish to try to predict the impact of the new China on Asia or the wider world; one need not necessarily accept the perhaps over-simplified theory that the policy of Peking (if there is such a thing in the present chaotic condition of the country) is military aggrandizement—let alone to "turn the Pacific into a Communist lake". Indeed there are historic grounds for doubt on that score—and there is a tendency to overlook the factor of Japan, who will certainly again be a power to reckon with in that part of the world. But, however that may turn out, there is unfortunately one fact of life which is enough to make it certain that tension and turbulence in Asia is the prospect before us for years to come, and that is the Asian population explosion: the present figures more than doubled in the next forty years, if a United Nations estimate is anything to go by. Even now, millions in Asia are undernourished and the spectre of famine is never far in the background.

In the West the prospect of all-out nuclear war between the Soviet Union and the Nato Powers—if it ever really existed—has obviously receded. Both the Colossi have huge stocks of nuclear weapons—a Devil's armoury which, if it were ever to be unleashed, would mean the end of civilization—perhaps even of life on earth by dimming the sun's rays and plunging this planet into another Ice Age that could last a thousand years or more. But both seem now to understand that, and indeed, especially since the Cuba crisis, are inclined to avoid any direct clash that could lead to it; the emergence of China as a nuclear Power is clearly a factor here. Both, however, are still bitterly at loggerheads and the Russians are in fact waging a different kind of war, largely by proxy—fishing in every troubled water, backing everyone (except China) who is or can be an enemy or embarrassment to the Western Powers, and supplying arms to anyone who can be trusted to use them irresponsibly. The old historic Nations of Europe are still divided by the great schism of which the shameful symbol is the Berlin Wall. And in Western Europe itself the hopeful trend towards Europeanism and the Atlantic ideal has been brutally halted—one must hope

only temporarily—by the paranoiac chauvinism of an aged
Frenchman and the lack of guts in most French politicians.

★   ★   ★

All this may seem to add up to a grisly catalogue of horrors—
a Himalayan mass of looming dangers and immeasurable
difficulties. But no one should lose heart. Things have been bad
before and are never as bad as they look—and it is only the
horrors that are 'News'. It is up to the young—not least to the
young of Britain. It is no good their just growing their hair
long and blaming everything on their elders. They are beginning their useful lives in a very different world. I hope they
will have the sense to profit by the mistakes of their forebears, but also the charity to acknowledge their immense
achievements.

> "Thrones, Powers, Dominions, Peoples, Kings,
> Are changing 'neath our hand;
> Our fathers also see these things
> But they do not understand."[7]

Maybe they do not; but they are not all such fools as some like
to make out. There is much virtue in the old ways; and new
ways are not necessarily superior just because they are new.
One unchanging truth is that nothing worth doing is ever
accomplished without some self-sacrifice and some work
beyond the call of duty or the scope of the pay-packet. And
remember, the one all-embracing virtue is kindness.

These dangers *can* be overcome, the difficulties surmounted.
"All that is necessary for evil to prevail is that good men do
nothing";[8] good men—and there are plenty of them (though
we in this country are in rather a thin bin just at the moment)—
will *not* do nothing. Nuclear war can be prevented; the technological Frankenstein can be made to remain man's servant

[7] *Our Fathers Also* by Rudyard Kipling.
[8] Edmund Burke.

and need never be his master; the extremes of nationalism and racialism need not prevail; great imaginative projects like the Mekong Delta scheme could feed and sustain countless millions; victory over the deadly diseases is not impossible and the world's birth-rates could be controlled; the sea could be tapped for its inexhaustible supplies of food. All these triumphs and more are attainable by free men and women with energy and guts, imagination and compassion.

*   *   *

But what is to be the role of the British people in that salvation?

Well—at the one extreme, we certainly cannot go it alone—no nation can, not even the United States. At the other, we can pin no hopes on the United Nations Organization for this purpose in the foreseeable future. I do not under-rate U.N.O.—it may be a talking shop, but that is better than a fighting shop; "Jaw Jaw is better than War War" as Churchill used to say, and U.N.O. may at least help to educate all these little new nations in some of the realities of international life—though it seems to be taking a long time about it. But if we imagine that there is the remotest possibility as far ahead as we need look of anything in the nature of World Government, we merely delude ourselves.

But there can and must be something between the two extremes. In January of 1962 a hundred representatives of the Allied Powers (of whom I was one) nominated by and instructed to report to their Governments, assembled in the Atlantic Convention of Nato Nations. The outcome of their deliberations was the "Declaration of Paris", which included a unanimous recommendation that the Allied Governments should initiate immediate action to develop N.A.T.O. and O.E.C.D.[9] into a true Atlantic Community with its own institutions—Consultative Assembly, High Court and so on—of which the primary object should be to "harmonize political, military and economic policy on matters affecting the Com-

[9] The Organization for Economic Co-operation and Development.

munity as a whole". If our Governments had acted on that recommendation instead of merely paying lip-service to it (or throwing it in the fire, as de Gaulle did a year later), we could by now have had at least the beginnings of a system whereby we could agree upon the general lines of a practical working consensus of Allied policy towards just the sort of massive problems that plague the world today. I must resist the temptation to inflict upon readers a treatise on a subject which has occupied so much of my time and attention in recent years. So I will only say that it is an article of faith with me that the future for Britain lies in playing a leading part in this Atlantic community. And it *could* be a leading part; but if we are to fill it, we shall have to do a good deal better than we have done in the past decade.

*   *   *

Among the very few really great men of our time was Field-Marshal Smuts, and one of my proudest claims is that I was privileged to be a friend of his. I saw him last at his home at Doornkloof less than a year before his death, and talked with him in his study, that big book-lined room which had once been the anteroom of a British Infantry Mess. One thing he said to me then has always stuck in my mind; "Never forget," he said, "that if England is true to herself, she can have an influence on American policy out of all proportion to her material or physical strength."

I was to recall those words some years later at what I think was, in public affairs, the blackest moment of my experience—and I have lived through a few black moments. I had the misfortune to arrive by air in Washington on the evening of the day on which Eden made his announcement in the Commons of the Suez "ultimatum"; and next morning was told on the telephone that "an old wartime friend of mine" wished to see me in the White House that afternoon. I am still not sure why Eisenhower sent for me; I think he probably felt that he just had to blow off steam on an old British friend in a position of no responsibility. Anyway, when he had blown off his steam and at last asked me what I thought of it all, I said I was not really capable at the moment of connected thought on the subject, but that there were two things to which I had devoted a great deal of my time and energy since leaving the Air Staff four years before—the Commonwealth and the Anglo-American alliance—and I was terribly afraid that our action had put both in mortal jeopardy.

As it turned out, my worst fears were not realized—or not to anything like the extent that then seemed probable. But I tell this story by way of illustration, as an example of an occasion when England was *not* true to herself. The Suez affair was the nadir of British statesmanship; it was not only a colossal political blunder and a military muddle—as the events of June 1967 surely proved, if proof was needed. It was also ethically indefensible in my view—and I knew a bit about what had been going on. For me it was impossible not to feel that some virtue had gone out of England. I had known British Governments to act weakly and stupidly before—sometimes with almost criminal stupidity—but never dishonourably. True, we later retrieved our position to some extent, and the end result was not as catastrophic as it might have been—thanks largely to Harold MacMillan, to give him his due; but it was disastrous enough in all conscience: it squandered far more than we could afford of our "capital of respect for [Britain's] wisdom, maturity, moderation and skill".[10]

The Nassau agreement that came some years later was not dishonourable—though I think the manner in which the business was handled left a great deal to be desired, to say the least of it; but it was an idiocy. And we cannot afford to be either dishonourable or idiotic in our conduct of Foreign Affairs if we are to assume and retain the role that is our due in the Atlantic Community which is our hope for the future. It would be an evil day, not only for us British but for the world, if the time ever came when foreigners did not believe that our word is to be trusted. Even as I write, there are grounds for some

[10] *The Diplomacy of the Great Powers* by Sir William Haytor.

anxiety on that score. In February 1966 we announced to the world in the Defence Review that the Atlantic Alliance is "vital to our survival"; in June we pledged ourselves in Brussels to maintain adequate forces in Europe for Deterrence and Defence; in July—under pressure of an economic crisis of our own making—we threatened to pull our troops out of Europe unless the Germans write us a cheque; I wonder if that is really a way a great Nation ought to behave. Again, our decision to leave South Arabia, while refusing any really worthwhile agreement to come to the help against external attack after our withdrawal of those who succeed us, always smelt too much like betrayal for my comfort; and by the time these words appear in print we may see utter chaos in that part of the world and another humiliating defeat for British policy. I have a nasty feeling that there are men in Bonn and Washington, certainly in the Middle and perhaps by now even in the Far East and Australasia, who have come to some pretty unpleasant conclusions about what British pledges are worth.

It is true that to some extent we do seem still to understand that we are not entitled to expect the United States to carry alone the whole burden of responsibility for the protection of Western interests from Port Said to the Pacific. We are, in my view, running down our military strength overseas too much and too fast. But we have not yet fully accepted the blandishments of the Little Englanders—those curious people who want us to save hard currency by ratting on our Treaty Commitments and moral obligations to friends and Commonwealth partners East of Suez; they do not seem to have quite the same inhibitions about spending it on imports that we could produce ourselves, more expensively perhaps, but by British workers in our own factories—and anyway for a fraction of what we now squander on bingo and betting, liquor and lipstick.

This is not a lecture on strategic policy, and by the time this book sees the light of day much of what I have said will have been overtaken by events. I only mention these things to hammer home a vital principle—that material prosperity is not everything; that there are some things more important in life than motor-cars and washing machines and T.V. sets—and one of them is the honour of Britain.

*   *   *

Let me sum up what I have been trying to say in this Epilogue, which it would be presumptuous—and unduly pompous—to describe as a philosophy of life for the rising generation.

In Foreign Affairs we should not be satisfied until we have secured our proper place in Europe, and seen at least the beginnings of a true Atlantic Community. We must be loyal to our Allies, must do our duty (which at the same time serves our self interest) as a member of N.A.T.O., and pull our due weight in maintaining order and stability in the Third World. We must work untiringly for peace and international understanding, unhampered by outworn traditions, free of racial prejudice, but without surrender of vital principles. We must meet our moral obligations—which again will serve our own interest—by devoting the appropriate share (and it is a big one) of our human and material resources to relieving the distress and forwarding the economic and political development of less fortunate peoples overseas. And in doing all these things we must never again forget that there are certain moral and ethical standards below which we fall at our peril.

If we conduct our affairs on these lines in the wider world; if at the same time here at home we really take the trouble and accept the sacrifices necessary to preserve and nourish the blessings we already enjoy; if we encourage enterprise in commerce and industry, while stamping out what remains of real poverty and squalor—and that, in relative terms, is not very much; if we work hard as well as playing hard, not trying to pay ourselves more than we earn—then we shall have nothing to fear. And our country once again will be as Smuts described her twenty-four years ago,[11] "Great Britain, with a glory and an honour and a prestige such as perhaps no Nation has ever

[11] Speech to the Empire Parliamentary Association, 1943.

enjoyed in history; recognized as possessing a greatness of soul that has entered into the very substance of World history."

So "say not the struggle nought availeth". Struggle is a condition of life and nothing worth doing ever has or ever will be done without it. "There is a tide in the affairs of men" and for the young this is an intensely interesting and exciting time to live in. Some of us older ones may perhaps be forgiven for feeling sometimes that it is a bit too exciting—that we have had enough excitement in the past fifty years to be going on with. But our grandsons and their contemporaries will never be able to complain that there is nothing worth while for them to do. I have enough faith in youth to believe that they will not fail us, and Britain will again be Great.

> "For while the tired waves, vainly breaking
> Seem here no painful inch to gain,
> Far back, through creeks and inlets making
> Comes silent, flooding in, the main."[12]

---

[12] A. H. Clough.

Postcript

The epilogue was first written in November 1966 and slightly amended a year later. No essay on the contemporary international or domestic scene can possibly, in these days, ever be completely up-to-date by the time it is published in a book. And now that another twelve months have passed I do not think it worthwhile attempting further amendment, which would again probably be out of date by the time this book appears in print. So I will leave my readers to amuse themselves (perhaps hardly an appropriate expression) by reflecting how and to what extent it has been overtaken by events at the time they come to read it.

That will certainly give them something to think about—not much to their comfort I'm afraid. First and foremost they must consider the implications of the unspeakably treacherous rape of Czecho-Slovakia by the granite-faced tyrants of the Kremlin. They should reflect on the epidemic of "student" unrest, and the revolt against established authority in so many countries; on the Paris conference about Vietnam and developments in that unhappy country; on the probable results of Mr. Nixon's election as President of the United States; on the Pope's extraordinary encyclical on birth control; on the horrible civil war in Nigeria and the deadlock over Rhodesia; on the declared intention of our present Government to withdraw from East of Suez, the political and economic implications of that decision, and its effects on our Armed Forces—particularly on the Army.

On the face of it, this world is a frightening place to live in; it would be silly to deny that it has become more so in the past

decade or two—a result of the scientific and technological as
well as the social and racial revolutions through which the
world is passing. But it is important to nourish a sense of
perspective. I am not sure whether that is more difficult for
younger people, who are coming to maturity in the present
world climate, or for someone like me whose grandfather (who
died when I was fifteen and of whom I was always a little
afraid) was born only six years after the Battle of Waterloo, in
which his father had commanded a battalion. Anyway, the
fact surely is that the world always has been a pretty frightening place if only we—or our predecessors—had known it.
Today a prime cause of unease is that anything that happens
anywhere in the world is immediately reflected in our headlines and on our T.V. screens—especially if it is horrific and
sensational—regardless of its intrinsic importance. It is News.
I wonder what our forebears would have felt a hundred years
ago if the realities could have been brought into their comfortable sitting-rooms of, say, the Irish famines, the Commune
in Paris, or the appalling conditions of life for the industrial
proletariat in the mines and mills of England and the almost
utter lack of social conscience among all but a very few (like
Lord Ashley) who could have changed them. While overseas,
the Indian Mutiny, the war between the States in America,
the endless civil strife in China, and the rubber atrocities in
the Congo would surely have looked pretty terrifying on
"Panorama".

Without going back as far as that, recent disorders in our
streets and universities had their somewhat similar parallels in
the Mosleyite hooliganism of the middle thirties.

So let no one lose heart. 1967 and 1968 have been unpleasant years on any reckoning. But it is sheer defeatism to
imagine that these conditions will continue indefinitely. While
avoiding complacency like the plague, we must keep our heads
and not give way to pessimism or cynical indifference. We
must look behind the sensational headlines and form our own
opinions. The world's tragedies and follies are a challenge to

younger generations which I believe they will meet and overcome. They must do so, not by endless reaching for more and
more material prosperity at the expense of other people—we
have already more than our fair share of that in a world context; certainly not by being a violent nuisance in the streets to
peaceable citizens and our long-suffering police; but by culti-
vating a sober awareness of what is really wrong and a quiet
determination to put it right—at some sacrifice to themselves.
This, perhaps, is *the* great challenge to our system of education.
At home, the major task seems to me to be the really drastic
improvement in management and labour relations that is
indispensable if we are to continue to enjoy the advantages to
which we have become accustomed, and take the place which
is our due in a European—and ultimately an Atlantic—Community. Overseas, our influence is unfortunately but inevitably
far less than it used to be. But we British can still have a far-
reaching impact on world affairs, not by yelling outside the
American Embassy, but by taking the trouble to understand
what is going on and why, and when possible by getting out
into the world, getting to know these people in Asia and
Africa, working among and with them and making the necessary sacrifices to reduce the appalling gap between their
standards of living and our own—which is as much in our
long-term interest as in theirs.

We must understand that, in the words of Barbara Ward,[1]
the earth has become a planetary village, and the need for us to
observe—world wide—the basic rules of community life is one
of the most profound, social and moral facts of our age.

Goodness knows that is not going to be easy; but nothing
worth doing is ever easy.

Nov. 1968

[1] Address to the English Speaking Union in Edinburgh, July 1968.